My Groupon Adventure

Max Dickins

unbound

This edition first published in 2016

Unbound
6th Floor, Mutual House, 70 Conduit Street, London W1S 2GF

Typeset by PDQ

Art direction by Mecob

NP: While every effort has been made to trace the owners of copyright material reproduced herein, the publisher would like to apologise for any omissions and will be pleased to incorporate missing acknowledgments in any further editions.

A CIP record for this book
is available from the British Library

ISBN 978-1-78352-260-6 (trade pbk)
ISBN 978-1-78352-262-0 (ebook)
ISBN 978-1-78352-281-1 (limited edition)

Printed in Great Britain by Clays Lts, St Ives Plc

1 2 3 4 5 6 7 8 9

*For Mum & Dad. See? I didn't totally
waste a good education.*

Dear Reader,

The book you are holding came about in a rather different way to most others. It was funded directly by readers through a new website: **Unbound**.

Unbound is the creation of three writers. We started the company because we believed there had to be a better deal for both writers and readers. On the Unbound website, authors share the ideas for the books they want to write directly with readers. If enough of you support the book by pledging for it in advance, we produce a beautifully bound special subscribers' edition and distribute a regular edition and e-book wherever books are sold, in shops and online.

This new way of publishing is actually a very old idea (Samuel Johnson funded his dictionary this way). We're just using the internet to build each writer a network of patrons. Here, at the back of this book, you'll find the names of all the people who made it happen.

Publishing in this way means readers are no longer just passive consumers of the books they buy, and authors are free to write the books they really want. They get a much fairer return too – half the profits their books generate, rather than a tiny percentage of the cover price.

If you're not yet a subscriber, we hope that you'll want to join our publishing revolution and have your name listed in one of our books in the future. To get you started, here is a £5 discount on your first pledge. Just visit unbound. com, make your pledge and type **adventure** in the promo code box when you check out.

Thank you for your support,

Dan, Justin and John
Founders, Unbound

A note from the author

Hi guys,

My name is Max Dickins and this is the true story of how Groupon changed my life: firstly, everything I describe in the following pages genuinely happened. I wish it hadn't: as you'll see most of it is horrifically embarrassing. Secondly, all the people I meet along the way are real – although I have changed various names when required to protect their privacy and, in one particular case, to stop them from coming after me with an axe.

In this book I'm going to tell you how I learnt to be adventurous. I am a stand-up comedian by trade. You probably think that doing stand-up is as adventurous as it gets. Onstage, in the bear pit atmosphere of a comedy club, I was brave and audacious. But offstage I was the opposite. My life was boring. I never did anything new. I never took a risk. I was the antithesis of spontaneity. Until I found Groupon, that is.

Thanks for taking a chance on my book. If there is one thing that writing it has taught me, it's that brilliant adventures often begin in such blind faith. And I hope this book inspires you to change your life as I changed mine. I've written it for anyone who has ever felt stuck in a rut, who has felt like their life is missing some excitement, who has felt like they're not living life to the full. I hope you enjoy it.

Yours,
Max

Chapter One

'I don't love you anymore,' she said. Jen couldn't look me in the eye; instead she stared at the floor and played with her hands. 'I'm sorry. But I think we should break up.' I shuffled slightly on the cold wooden bench and gazed off intensely into the middle distance. I had not seen this coming. For the next few minutes we sat in silence. Finally, Jen spoke again:

'I can't believe you've dressed up as Batman.'

'I thought … I thought it would be funny. You know, like a wacky surprise.'

'It's really inappropriate.'

'Well, I didn't know you were going to dump me, did I?'

Jen had ditched me and she'd chosen to do it in a cemetery. So, although devastated, I couldn't help but admire her inherent sense of motif. She was the Steven Spielberg of break-ups. The only way the symbolism could have been any more apt was if a mangy old Rottweiler walked into view chewing on a beating heart. 'But … why Jen? Baby! We've never had a row … I don't understand?' Yes, I called her 'Baby'. I admit it. It was one of many pet names I had for her at the time, including 'Honey', 'Sugar Plum', and 'The Fat Controller'. She hated that one. Jen had nicknames for me too. Notably 'Sledgehammer' and 'Mega Cock'.

Jen looked awkwardly at the floor again. 'I just don't feel

like I did. I'm sorry.' My eyes felt like they were burning. But I didn't want to cry because I was dressed as Batman and I'd just look like a 'Fathers for Justice' protester. I promised myself that whatever happened I would leave this conversation with my dignity intact. I wasn't going to get hysterical and make an idiot of myself. No way. I wasn't going to give her the satisfaction.

'PLEASE PLEASE PLEASE PLEASE DON'T LEAVE ME! I'll do anything! JEN *I CAN CHANGE*! PLEASE DON'T LEAVE ME! Tell me! What did I do wrong?'

She rolled her eyes. 'Max don't …' she said, 'please'. 'No, tell me. What's the problem? Is it because of that time I made your blind uncle stroke an aubergine and told him it was a dolphin?'

'I didn't know you did that.'

'Oh … right … ummm … is it because I tried to kiss your mum last New Year's Eve?'

'I didn't know that either'.

'Oh … shit, well, I was really drunk … and I thought we were having a moment, but it turned out she was just offering me some crisps … forget about it. But if not that, then what? WHAT'S WRONG WITH ME? AM I REALLY SUCH A DISGUSTING *LEPER*!'

Jen paused to gather her thoughts. 'Well if you must know … you're just not very *spontaneous*,' she said. Then, ironically, I spontaneously burst into tears. At this point a young boy came over with his mother, who asked whether her son could have a photo with Batman. I nodded with resignation, put my arm around the lad, and his mum did the rest. The boy clocked my sobs.

'Why are you crying, Batman?'

'Because Robin doesn't want to play with me anymore,' I said.

'I'll play with you, Batman?'

'No. That would be inappropriate.'

The boy was then led off urgently by his mother, who shook her head at me like I had somehow let her down. As if introducing a child to a man crying in a cemetery, whilst dressed as a bat, was ever going to end well. I composed myself long enough to look Jen in the eye and plead, 'I'm still the same person you fell in love with, you know?' 'Exactly,' she said, 'that's the problem.' Then she kissed me on the cheek and walked away. On cue, it started to rain. I don't know how she does it.

I trudged back from the cemetery to my parents' house where, at 25 years of age, I was still living. I shut myself in my room and for the next fortnight I barely left. I retreated from the world, anchored indoors by the heavy scar tissue of a broken heart. Marooned in existential molasses, I spent all my time alone, trapped in an internet labyrinth of tits and trivia. Things were bleak. I vividly remember accidentally opening the 'Recently Searched' tab on my internet browser one day, and it was the most depressing thing I'd ever read, a harrowing glimpse into my life at the time:

Porn.

Porn.

Porn.

Porn.

Theresa May.

Theresa May porn.

Then the names of loads of celebrities, followed by the word 'bikini'.

And finally, *'How much Colgate would I have to eat to kill myself?'*

Jen would still text me and, of course, I'd always play it cool. Replying at length and immediately, often including poetry. I was happy to be an emotional tampon if it kept alive the possibility of spending one more second with her. We'd regularly meet for coffee and chat about how great it was that we were so chilled about things and how we'd both dealt with the change so well. Then I'd go home and eat lasagne in the bath.

This lasted about three weeks. Then one day there was a knock on my bedroom door. I quickly slammed down the lid of my laptop as my best mate Dave barreled into the room. '*Wassssuuuuup!*' he said, tongue lolling like a dehydrated Labrador. Dave's been doing that joke for as long as I've known him. Including a good 10 years after it stopped being funny. 'Alright, Dave. What are you doing here?' 'Well,' said Dave, 'I popped over to do your mum up the bum, and thought it would be churlish not to say hello while I was in the building.' 'That's very kind of you,' I said, 'It's good to see you.' 'What's up mate? You've been ignoring my texts?' he said, sitting down on my bed. Dave was now staring at the *Thunderbirds* bedspread. 'Oh, that's only on there while Mum washes my normal one,' I stuttered. 'Yeah? What's on your normal one?' 'The Manchester United 1998-1999 treble winning squad,' I said. My head bowed in shame. 'Where the hell have you been?' said Dave. 'No one's seen you for weeks?' 'Yeah, sorry mate,' I said, 'just had a lot on.' 'The guys all thought you were dead. We had a party and everything. With a piñata shaped like your head.' Classic Dave.

I explained everything. I told him about Jen, the Batman costume, and my subsequent sophomoric wallowing. 'She dumped you in a cemetery?' he said. 'Fair play!' Dave has many strengths but sympathy is not one of them. 'To be honest, mate, I'm surprised it lasted as long as it did. You were really punching above your weight there.' This was not helping. 'Is there another guy? Has she left you for someone taller and more successful?' 'I'm five feet nine, Dave!' 'Course you are, mate'. I told him about Jen's central charge, that I wasn't spontaneous enough. 'Absolutely bang on,' said Dave, 'You always say no to everything.'

'No, I don't!' I protested. 'Yes you do!' he said, 'Now do you want to come down karaoke with me and the boys tonight? It's a Bon Jovi special.' 'Errr … well … I can't tonight, I'm afraid, mate.' 'I rest my case,' said Dave, 'what have you got on? Are BBC4 showing a documentary about biscuits or something?' I let out an indignant chortle. As if I'd pull out of a social occasion to watch a documentary about biscuits! Just how dull did he think I was? No, it was actually an excellent programme about the world's longest bridges.

Another month passed. Then, on 13th November 2013 my 26th birthday, everything changed. That morning I'd gone to Costa with Jen, you know, so she could tell me about how great her life was now. And as we awkwardly sipped our lattes she asked me the question that she always asked me. '*So! What's new with you?*' And I had nothing to say. I never had anything to say. I hadn't done anything new in years. I always saw the same people, in the same places, to do the same things. I hadn't done anything new because doing something new requires a sense of adventure and I've never had one. Not even when I was a kid. Children are meant to be fearless, excited, and energetic. But here I am, five years old, sat on the beach:

Am I looking for crabs? Swimming in the sea? Building sandcastles, even? No, I'm sat by myself, reading the financial pages, dressed as a sailor. Twenty-one years later that boy had become a man and not much had changed. I was still basically the same height, I still had the same dress sense, and I was still boring. What was really galling was that my parents, despite both being in their sixties, had much more of a life than I did. For example, on my 26th birthday, whilst I was sat at home all alone doing nothing, my parents were on holiday in Nepal:

There they are. Pricking about with an elephant. Whilst I was stranded on their sofa watching a Miss Marple marathon. But the worst part of my birthday was about ten o'clock in the morning, when I got this text from Mum:

'Oh Happy Birthday Max! PS If you look in the freezer, you'll find a frozen walnut cake.'

So I went and got the frozen walnut cake out of the freezer, put it on the table, and I waited all day for a frozen birthday cake to defrost. And then I ate the entire cake. The only way that day could have gone any worse for me, was if, at the bottom of the cake, on the foil, my parents had just written 'YOU ARE ADOPTED'. Do you know how depressing it is to light your own candles? This is pretty much the loneliest thing I've ever done. Apart from a few days previously when I'd put a wig on a watermelon and pretended I had an intern called Sophie.

I looked in my diary. That evening I had a gig. I thought, 'That will be nice. I'll do the gig, hang out with the other comics afterwards, have a few drinks. It will be fun.' But at five o'clock in the afternoon on my birthday the gig was cancelled, and I thought, 'Well, I can't spend any more time by myself on my birthday'. So I went to the cinema (by myself) to watch the film *Gravity*. I don't know if you've ever seen *Gravity*, but in *Gravity* Sandra Bullock floats all alone through the depths of space, just staring into the abyss, and I have never felt more like I understood a film. As the credits rolled at the end of that movie I decided: enough is enough. I'd reached rock-bottom: I needed to get a life. I had to change, but I didn't know how. So I called Dave.

Two hours later I was sat in Wetherspoon's with a pint in my hand. I looked around the pub. A sallow cast of old men stared vacantly up at ubiquitous flat-screens incongruently showing BBC News. The flashing lights of the fruit machines visible in the dark pools of their eyes, like fireworks reflecting off a lake. Tonight was Curry Club, but there was little team spirit on show. Everyone was drinking alone, but no one was talking to one another. Instead, choosing to feign a deep interest in the Greek financial crisis unfolding above them. I took a long, mournful sip of lager: was this my future? Dave, however, was in a great mood. He'd just been to a Vengaboys reunion gig at the O2 Arena, and was carrying a big blue inflatable Venga Bus. (Dave's tastes, like his cultural references, hadn't changed since the late 90s. It's like the Y2K bug affected *only* him.) 'I don't know what to do, Dave. My life's so boring,' I said. 'No. No. Your life's not boring,' he said. 'Yes it is!' I said, 'I've spent most of the day playing Monopoly by myself!' 'No. No. No: YOU'RE boring, mate. Only boring people have a boring life.' This was very on the nose even for Dave. But he was already on his fifth Baileys, to be fair.

'A boring life, right? A boring life … is the result of taking certain decisions, it's the result of looking at the world in a certain way, yeah?' Dave was holding court like a pissed Yoda, gesticulating wildly with his glass, inadvertently spilling Baileys all over the table. 'You've just got to teach yourself to look at the world differently, to trust in the universe, yeah?' 'What the fuck are you talking about, Dave?' I said. 'Well, like, for example, last week I went to the S Club 7 comeback tour at the Hammersmith Apollo. People told me it would be crap. That Jo and the lads were over the hill. But I took a chance, I asked myself "Why not?" I thought: "This might be brilliant, let's not die wondering." And I went and it was the best night of my entire life. *My entire life.* And I include the night my son was born in that,' he said. 'You haven't got a son, Dave. The Sims isn't real.' 'Look, you can nitpick if you want. I haven't got time for your sterile pedantry. But it's like this, OK? Forget about your fears tonight. Listen to your heart. Let's just touch the sky, no need to reason why. Just listen to the sound. Let it make you come alive.' 'Dave, is that an S Club 7 lyric?' 'Exactly. "Don't Stop Movin". An all-time classic. Now if you will excuse me, I must go and be sick.' And with that Dave stood up and made for the toilet, falling over his Venga Bus on the way.

Annoyingly, Dave was right. Not about 'Don't Stop Movin' 'being an all-time classic – that was clearly a heinous misjudgement – but about my life. I had to teach myself to take a risk. I needed a sea change in how I was living and to do that I needed to change how I thought about the world. I needed an entirely new psychology. It was a tall order, but if I could teach myself to be spontaneous then perhaps I could win back the love of my life. After all, I still believed that we could make it work. It was just a blip. We were so well matched. I just needed to re-invent myself, to prove that I could grow with her and keep things interesting. Then she would fall in love with me all over again. I was sure of it.

The very next day I got this text from Dave:

'Fancy seeing Five at the Hackney Empire? Might cheer you up. Cheap tickets on Groupon.'

Obviously I had no interest in doing that. I'd had my heart ripped out, not my brain. But, still, I was intrigued: what the hell was *Groupon*? So I googled it and found this parallel universe of eccentric and exciting offers. On the front page alone were *'Helicopter Flying Lessons'*, *'Ferrari Driving Experience'*, and *'Wakeboarding'*. My stomach flipped. Suddenly I realised that Groupon could be my ladder out of my rut. It was spontaneity for beginners. A simple menu of adventures and all I had to do was order. This Narnia of discounts had suddenly made the universe feel full of possibility again. I felt energised; perhaps I could change my life one Groupon deal at a time? But still I couldn't bring myself to take the first step. My cursor hovered hesitantly over the 'Buy' button. All of a sudden I felt nervous. Pathetic excuses dressed up as faultless logic rebounded around my mind: 'It's too expensive', 'I'll look like an idiot', 'I've got no-one to do it with'. But I knew these arguments were simply *no* in a tuxedo. My subconscious was desperately searching for a way out. I just couldn't see myself as *'that guy'* who would do these mad things. I shut my laptop and made myself a jam sandwich.

That evening I got another text from Mum:

'Just been skydiving LOL! It was amazing. But you'd probably hate it haha x'

And I felt weirdly angry. I was irritated that own mother had assumed I would hate skydiving. Is that how people saw me? As some sort of pathetic old codger? I wanted to confound them. I realised that although I wasn't that crazy, spontaneous guy yet I could fake it till I made it. It would be like method acting. I'd just read a book about it. Stanislavski called it the 'Magic If'. If you want to play the part of someone who is sad, act 'as if' you were sad and then you will become it. I'd just have to play the part of a spontaneous guy until it became second nature. So I didn't need to believe I was adventurous to behave with adventure. I just had to *do* it. The cast iron belief would appear eventually in the rear-view mirror. This was an empowering epiphany. Now I just had to get on with it. It was time to take a deep breath and step off the cliff. Groupon had made it easy. I'd found my tool, my portal to a better life and I steeled myself to begin my journey. But I wanted to break myself into this wonderful new world slowly. Helicopters and wakeboarding seemed a bit extreme to me. And so when I saw '*Acupuncture and Massage*' come up, I thought: 'This is much more my scene'.

Chapter Two

My first Groupon was at a place called 'Oriental Healthcare', which boasted it was 'London's oldest exponent of the ancient art of Chinese medicine'. You'd probably expect that to be in Chinatown, wouldn't you? But no, it was in Romford. The Chinese doctor welcomed me in warmly. His name was Ken and he spoke with a really strong cockney accent. Unless he was screaming abuse at his wife, when he used a barrage of Chinese gibberish. I sat in the reception area and sipped tea out of a chipped mug in the shape of Prince Charles's head. There was a framed faded photo of the snooker player Ronnie O'Sullivan on the grubby wall. On the dirty coffee table in front of me lay a thumbed copy of *Take a Break* magazine from 2003. The headline read: 'My husband is a dog'. Ken sat down next to me, a little too close, grinning the sort of smile you might throw a coconut through at the fairground. It was as if he couldn't believe he had an actual customer.

'Is acupuncture dangerous?' I asked nervously. 'Who have you been talking to?' he said, angrily. 'Look, it was a mistake. If anything he's walking *more*.' I smiled tensely. 'This acupuncture guff is a piece of piss!' he said, through saffron yellow teeth. 'So don't be scared! Anyway, 'ave you seen the guest book?' I had seen the guest book, and it was impressive: testimonial after testimonial from delighted

11

clients, all written in the same handwriting. Finally, Ken began the consultation. He took my pulse, and then asked me to show him my tongue, so I poked it out, and he just stared at it and shook his head. Then he scribbled something on his form in Chinese writing. Well I think it was Chinese writing, it was hard to tell: he might have been drawing a tiny picture of a cat.

Next, Ken led me into a small dark room that smelt of spoiled meat. He asked me to take my clothes off and lie face down on the bed. So I got totally naked and clambered into position on the sheets, which felt oddly moist, like a used hanky. Ken re-entered 'Why have you taken your pants off?' 'You told me to get undressed?' I said. 'Yeah, but obviously keep your pants on, you doughnut! What sort of place do you think this is? We're from Shanghai, not Bangkok. But I suppose we all look the same to you do we?' Ken left again. I put on my boxers. Ken returned and started filling my back up with needles. Acupuncture, it turns out, is pretty painful. Especially if the bloke doing it thinks you're a racist pervert.

Acupuncturists believe that illness is caused by an imbalance in our life energy, or '*qi*' (pronounced 'chee'). Acupuncture is meant to unblock the flow of this energy around our body. And if acupuncture wasn't my cup of *qi*, then Ken's subsequent gambit certainly wasn't either. The next treatment was called 'cupping', which was nothing to do with testicles, thank God. Ken stuck a load of jam jars on my back, but having first burnt out the oxygen with a candle, creating a vacuum that sucked up my skin. It's a bit like getting a love bite off a hoover (a friend has told me). As he did it, he said, 'This might leave a bit of a mark, but nothing serious, only for a couple of days'. This is what my back looked like two weeks later:

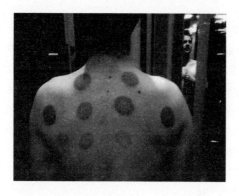

A BIT OF A MARK! I LOOK LIKE I'VE FALLEN ASLEEP ON THE HOB.

Anyway, jam jars removed, Ken told me to lie there and wait for the masseuse. I was nervous about the massage. I'd never had one before and I had one big worry: *what if I get an erection?* Crikey, that would be awkward, especially after Pantsgate. The masseuse came in. For some reason I assumed I'd have a lovely little Chinese lady. It turned out to be a massive Spanish bloke called Juan. Immediately my erection worries *trebled*. God, he was good, with his big Catalan hands; and so strong, riding me with his powerful thighs. I was in heaven. Anyway, he flipped me over and finished me off – not like that – lit a candle (nice touch), and with that disappeared off into the night like Zorro, without as much as a kiss goodbye. As if it meant nothing to him.

Having re-dressed, I wandered back to the reception area. Ken was there giving it the hard sell, like a fruit and veg man down Romford market:

'Juan's the dog's bollocks, isn't he?'

'Yes,' I said, 'terrific.'

'So I suppose you want to sign up for some more sessions?'

'Umm … to be honest, I'm a bit hard up at the moment.'

'Yes, Juan mentioned.'

'No, as in I haven't got any money.'

'Alright, twist me arm: I'll give you six sessions for the price of four and I'll throw in a bag of turtles' dicks for free?'

I politely declined. 'Would you like me to sign the guest book, Ken?' I said. 'Nah you're alright, we'll do that for you.'

I stepped into the bracing November air feeling refreshed, literally and metaphorically. For the first time in years I'd done something new and it was invigorating. I was being spontaneous! And I wanted to keep the momentum up. I knew what I was like: if I stopped, I'd never start again. I'd go back to square one: a dull man eating ready meals for two, alone, in front of Nazi documentaries. I decided to leap straight into my next adventure. I got home and immediately rolled the Groupon roulette wheel again. I landed on something completely bizarre – I went alpaca trekking in Kent.

Apparently in a car park. You'll notice I'm wearing an alpaca wool scarf, which is adding insult to injury for the alpaca. That's like going to meet a pig wearing a bacon bikini. In hindsight, I think the alpaca trek is aimed at children rather than twenty-six-year-old men. I know that because on the trek it was just me and a six-year-old girl. She turned up with her mother and her sister, but farm policy demanded that only two people could go on each trek and so the little girl ended up coming with me. The first thing I did was grooming. (The alpaca, I mean, not the six-year-old girl). Then we all went for a walk around the Romney Marsh: me, the girl, Hershey the alpaca, and our guide, Lara. The little girl was such a brat. She just wouldn't stop talking; I couldn't get a word in edgeways.

'Where's his mummy?'

'Do alpacas go to school?'

'Does he do a wee-wee or a poo-poo?'

All questions I wanted to ask, but couldn't. Alpacas are from the camel family. Their faces in particular seem impossibly fluffy, like a cloud with eyes, or a fat boy who's walked face first into a snowstorm. Their fleece is famously thick and soft but alpacas don't like you touching it. In fact, they don't like you at all. They're prey animals, meaning that where they evolved originally, on the cold mountains of Peru, everything was trying to eat them. Which makes them really jumpy: any sort of noise and they bolt. Hershey scared himself with his own fart and almost took my arm off. Alpacas are also extremely hierarchical animals and walk together in a straight line in a woolly conga. If anyone tries to get above their station and jump the queue they get spat at. Yes, literally spat at. Alpacas have two stomachs, like cows (and Americans), and they regurgitate green bile from the first chamber and gob it at you. I tell you what though: they can give it out but they can't take it. When I spat back at my alpaca it went absolutely mental.

But alpacas aren't just farmed to provide comic relief to bored

morons like me. They're also often used by farmers to scare off dogs and foxes. Alpacas hate dogs and if they corner one they jump on it until it dies, like canine bubble wrap. Not so cute now, are they? When the little girl heard that fact her face dropped, her naive world view shattered, as if she'd just walked in on her Barbie shooting-up smack. No wonder she was disappointed. We overly romanticise animals, I think, especially for children. But the truth is we are deluding ourselves if we think animals are ethical. Have you ever seen a nature documentary? Animals are nihilistic psychopaths. Dolphins are prolific rapists, female pigs often eat their own piglets, and pandas deliberately refuse to reproduce in a cynical attempt to get handjobs from humans.

We walked around the boggy fields for an hour or so, and a fun day ended with Lara presenting us with our certificates:

Lara also pinned a big badge on my chest, with the words 'Total Star' written on it, and then ruffled my hair for a bit. It was at this point that I realised Lara thought I had special needs.

The following lunchtime I'd arranged to meet Dave in the pub. 'Dave! I've fallen in love with Groupon! It's amazing!' 'Tell me about it mate,' he said. 'I've just bought two tickets to an Audience with Barry Manilow at the Royal Albert Hall for a tenner.' 'That's awesome, mate,' I replied with zero sincerity. 'So, are you going to keep going then?' he asked. 'Definitely, mate,' I said, 'I've decided I'm going to do one Groupon every week for a year.' Dave burst out laughing, a mist of lager expelled into the air by the strength of his guffaw. 'What's so funny?' I said. 'It's just I know you'll never do it! You won't follow through,' said Dave, wiping tears from his eyes. 'I bet I will,' I said. 'I bet you won't,' shot back Dave. 'Alright then, let's formalise this thing.' 'What do you mean? Draw up a legally binding contract?' 'Well maybe not a contract, but let's make this a proper bet with rules and stuff,' I said. 'Like what?' 'Well, I promise to do a Groupon every week for a year, up until my next birthday say, and if I do that then …' 'Then what?' 'Then I win and you have to give your awful CD collection to charity.' 'And if you fail, then what? What's the forfeit?' 'I won't fail.' 'But if you do? How about: if you fail then I'm allowed a crack at Jen.' 'What! No way!' 'Alright then, if you fail then me and the boys are allowed to choose a Groupon from Hell that you *have* to do. No ifs, no buts.' 'Deal,' I said. 'Deal,' he said. And we shook on it.

'Hang on,' said Dave. 'Do you get to choose the Groupons you do? What if you just choose nice stuff like haircuts and face peels?' Dave had a point. We needed to establish some more ground rules. So we decided that there were three laws I would abide by on 'My Groupon Adventure'. Firstly, as we'd just discussed, I would have to do an offer every week for a year. So that was 52 offers. I'd already done two, so I had only 50 more to go. Secondly, the Groupon deal at hand would have to be something that I'd never done before. Thirdly, Dave decreed that I must never take the easy option. No matter how well I'd got on with Juan there were to be no more massages. If I was really going to change myself, if I was to transform myself into this new monster of spontaneity, I would have to put in the hard yards. And that meant doing the weirdest deals I could lay my hands on. Dave was to be judge and jury of My Groupon Adventure. If Dave decided that I'd taken an easy option that would count as a failure and would invoke the Groupon Deal from Hell. 'And finally,' said Dave ominously, 'You cannot refuse a Groupon. If someone buys you a Groupon you are banned from saying no.' 'No problem,' I said. Because I could not imagine that ever being an issue. Who would buy me a Groupon? Nobody knew what I was up to and anyway, what sort of person would spunk 50 of their hard-earned pounds on a stupid activity just to make my life difficult? 'Deal,' I said again, shaking on it once more. And then Dave told me he'd bought me a voucher for dog yoga.

Dog yoga, or 'Doga', promised to allow me to access my dog on a 'more spiritual level'. This was a surprise to me. I was previously unaware that dogs had a spiritual level. In my experience, dogs tended to exist very much on a 'urinating on trees and sniffing each other's bum holes level'. But no. Apparently when dogs roll onto their backs and writhe about they don't want you to stroke their bellies. No, they are simply overcome with the existential consequences of living in a godless universe. However there was one major obstacle to my dog yoga plans: I didn't actually have a dog. I don't want a dog, mainly because I don't trust myself to keep it alive. I've got a poor record keeping things alive: Tamagotchis, basil plants, and plumbers have all died on my watch. Also, I've never understood the idea that dogs are a man's best friend. That's a pretty odd ideal of friendship. On that model, a friend is someone who can't speak, who you've got to feed, and whose shits you clean up. If a dog is your best friend then who are your other bezzies? 'Oh this is Dan, he's a baby. And this is Gloria, she's in a coma.'

Clearly I needed a dog for the session. I couldn't just put a fake moustache on my mum's cat. Not again. So I rang around all my friends. Two minutes later I'd spoken to everybody. No-one could help me out, including Dave who said that he *would* have let me borrow his pug, Shania Twain, but unfortunately Shania Twain was being wormed. I'd reached a dead end, there was only one option left. The absolute last resort: I called my uncle and asked him if I could borrow his Jack Russell, Marmite, for a few hours. He said 'Yes' before I could finish the question, because Marmite is mental. Genuinely mad. He never stops moving, leaping around all day long like a popcorn kernel in a hot pan. And he barks, and he licks, and he chews, and he digs, and he farts. He's a pinball with an anus.

I picked the dog up from my uncle's flat in Putney. He was waiting in the road as I pulled in, with Marmite already straining at the leash. I opened the back door to my Peugeot to let Marmite climb in. For once the dog was stationary, looking away nonchalantly. 'He doesn't like to go in the back,' advised my uncle. 'He likes to ride up front.' 'Oh does he?' I said 'And what radio station does he prefer?' I opened the passenger door and Marmite hopped on the seat, propped aloofly on his hind legs. My uncle handed me a small yellow bag. 'He's just been for a dump, but here's a bag just in case.' He then ran inside and locked the door before I could change my mind. We set off. I put Radio 1 on. Almost immediately Marmite pawed the radio and changed the station to Classic FM.

The Doga was taking place in a dance studio near Fulham Broadway tube station. There were three other dog owners waiting in the hallway outside our room. They were a mother and her adolescent daughter, replete with Cocker Spaniel and Maltese puppy; and a lady in her early thirties, with blonde highlights and pink leotard, flanked by a disgusting hound that looked like an animatronic beard. The dogs were predictably losing their minds, turning the narrow corridor into a canine Hadron Collider. We all exchanged amusing small talk about the looming absurdity. The blonde lady looked down at her dog and looked back up at me and said, 'He's not going to talk to me after this.' I stared back at her: 'Does he talk to you now?'

Suddenly we were joined by a gossiping army of yummy mummies, with their ski-holiday tans and their botoxed brows. This was no great surprise. I lived down the road and I'd always see them in local cafes with their children called things like 'Sebastian' and 'Goujoun'. And they'd order their ridiculous coffees: *Hello, can I have a super super super skinny latte please? So that's no coffee, no milk, and no cup.* And then they'd order a thing called a 'Babycino' for young Taramasalata. Babycinos wind me up. They're essentially coffee-free cappuccinos for your little darlings. They're unbelievably pretentious. And they cost about four quid. What's going on in the world? A cappuccino for a child? When I was a kid, if I wanted a drink, I'd give myself a nosebleed. If parents are giving their children that to drink, it makes you wonder what they're putting in their lunchboxes.

'Did you enjoy your packed lunch today, darling?'

'Not really, mother. The lobster bisque was too salty. And was that chorizo from Lidl?'

Finally our instructor – Shawna – arrived to let us into the studio, handsome muscles swelling proudly out of black Lycra, her thick tan adding prominence to her gleaming prosthetic teeth. She appeared to have a wig tucked under her arm, but on closer inspection it was actually a pathetic looking Shih Tzu. Shawna placed her substantial bag of tricks on a side table and handed out our yoga mats, which we placed on the floor in a circular pattern as if petals on a flower. Then something very strange happened. The dogs started urinating on the mats. Mine in particular came in for a special hosing. Everywhere I looked genitals gushed. 'Oh, this is totally normal,' reassured Shawna. 'It's territorial.' I looked down at my mat, which glistened blackly. 'Errr … shall I go and get some loo roll?' I wasn't going to do yoga submerged in piss. I wanted to access my dog on a more spiritual level but I drew the line at water sports. Shawna reached into her bag and pulled out J-cloths and a luminous yellow bottle of Flash.

With the urine mopped and the congregation sat cross-legged on their mats, we were ready to begin Doga. 'You are Yogi and Doggie,' she said. 'It's very important to ignore your dog, don't play with them or drag them in to you. Concentrate on your breathing, clear your mind and be in the moment, I promise your dogs will come to you when they're ready.' We began our breathing exercises. It's very hard to be in the moment, to experience oneness with the universe, when there are five dogs attacking each other a few feet from your face. 'Inhale … exhale,' continued Shawna, a consummate pro. She seemed totally unfazed by the spaniel that had taken a huge interest in her vagina. We started to go through the yoga poses. Marmite swarmed, licking me and poking me with his wet nose, causing me to breakdown in uncontrollable giggles. The spaniel was now trying to escape through the door using his head as a battering ram. The other dogs barked and bit each other. This was pointless.

'Now we are going to breathe like a dog,' said Shawna as if it was the most normal thing in the world. 'Raise your cheekbones and smile ... good ... now open your mouth and stick your tongue out ... now pant like a dog.' We all exchanged nervous looks but did as we're told. 'By breathing like a dog it allows us to vibrate with the same energy as our dogs.' The dogs were now frenzied. 'They're barking because they think we're dogs.' After five minutes of panting, we returned to the yoga positions. The dogs continued to wrestle. Finally, something snapped in Shawna and she stood up and picked up her dog, which was placid to her touch. She knelt into position again, her dog on its back in between her legs, spread out like dough, totally docile. The others dogs seemed to relax. 'Robbie is the leader ... it's all hierarchical. They will chill-out now.'

We continued the session and gently a miracle unfolded. As my heart rate lowered and my breathing slowed, Marmite came and sat with me. 'Kiss your dog. Massage him from the top of his head to the bottom of his spine – that will stimulate the parasympathetic nervous system, and massage his neck. Dogs, like humans, have a lot of tension in their necks.' Marmite became malleable. His eyelids grew heavy. He affectionately licked my hands. He lay on his back in front of me. He let me pick him up and hold him against my waist as I stood legs far apart, bending in the trikonsana pose. He even appeared to mouth the word 'namaste', but I could have been hallucinating. Inhaling urine fumes for two hours will do that to a man. Finally, I released him as we did some final breathing exercises and he retreated into a corner and fell asleep. I had somehow become the dog whisperer.

'We are one energy,' explained Shawna, 'I believe in oneness – if we are relaxed and in the moment, then our dogs will be relaxed.' It sounds mad, I know, but if a delinquent like Marmite can be tamed with the power of the mind then maybe there is something in it. I put Marmite on the lead without a struggle for the first time ever, thanked Shawna and left the studio. As we walked down the stairs and through the lobby Marmite appeared in a trance. Then, as soon as we got outside, he first tried to run after a bus, then urinated on a pram, and then tried to wrestle the stick off a blind man. Within two minutes we were back at square one.

The morning after dog yoga I bought 600 quids' worth of Groupons in one big kamikaze credit card spree. I was a marketer's dream: all Groupon had to do was e-mail me about it and I'd buy it. So high was I on the drug of spontaneity. Consequently, I'd just purchased 500 toilet rolls for absolutely no reason, an online pathologist course, and a romantic minibreak to Hull – an oxymoron if I'd ever heard one. I didn't even have anyone to go with. But although I may have been careering towards bankruptcy, I was having an amazing time. I was more engaged in the world than I'd ever been and I felt giddy. I found with each passing Groupon that I was getting better at enjoying myself again. I think emotions are like skills in that if you don't use them you lose them. If you don't kick a ball for years you forget how to do it and for me it was the same with joy. With every new Groupon it was like I was rewiring my brain for fun. For years I'd been sleepwalking through life and all of a sudden I felt alive: resuscitated by the oxygen of new experience. My spontaneity muscle was growing and with it my chances to win back Jen's heart. But I had a number of hurdles to overcome first. Including my next adventure, where, for a good while, I thought I was going to be murdered.

Chapter Three

My next Groupon was my most sophisticated yet. I went life drawing in a church hall near Bethnal Green. When I arrived at the venue, I was hugely relieved. Groupon had sent me the postcode and I'd spent 40 minutes walking around the dark streets of a council estate trying to find it, anxiously staring at Google maps on my phone, half expecting it to be a hoax. Terrified that I'd end up sat alone in a random pervert's kitchen as he posed naked on a chair. Or worse. At the end of one ghoulish cul-de-sac I became convinced that I was being lured into a honeytrap where I'd be stabbed, dismembered and then dumped in a canal. And that was to become a calling card of the Groupon experience: at some point you're guaranteed to think that you're going to die. You get what you pay for, I suppose.

Life drawing is famously difficult. But as with all my experiences, being good wasn't the point: the point was to try something new. I've never been into art. Going to art galleries had always been something I felt I *should* enjoy, but I'd just never got round to it. I always seemed to have better things on like binge drinking and being asleep. I wasn't a total philistine though. I did have some art on my bedroom wall, which I'm ashamed to say I bought in Ikea. It was a small black and white photo of some rocks. I can't remember why I bought it. I assume it's because it looked a bit moody – moody is normally shorthand in culture for intelligent and complex. I wanted to be thought intelligent and complex, ergo, I bought a photo of some rocks.

I am embarrassed that I ever owned those rocks. If you buy art from Ikea you should not be allowed to leave the car park. There should be snipers on the roof that fire darts full of sedative into your neck as you attempt to leave the shop. Then you should wake up in a cold warehouse and be forced to build flat-pack furniture with only the Japanese version of the instructions and a few crucial bits missing until you go mad and kill yourself with an Allen key. Like a Swedish version of the film *Saw*. Because art should be an expression of you, surely? If that whole complex cathedral of self can be serviced by something as homogenous as Ikea then you are essentially dead inside. Having said that, you can furnish an entire five bedroom house for 12 quid, so you know, it's swings and roundabouts.

For the first time I'd managed to convince Dave to do a Groupon with me. We travelled separately but somehow arrived almost simultaneously. The organiser greeted us genially and directed us to the materials stacked up on a bench at the back of the room. There were paper, pencils, charcoals, and easels. Ten or so other people had already taken their places. Tables had been arranged in a large square formation, leaving a sizable space in the middle where the model stood in his open dressing gown sipping a cup of tea nonchalantly. Our model was a rotund bald man whose bulbous eyes stared out through thick-lensed glasses. He looked like a studious egg. Paul was about forty years old, with a pot belly hanging over a substantial member, shadowing it like those patio awnings retired policemen sell to vulnerable old women on daytime TV. The organiser, himself an artist, said that Paul would do a variety of poses for us to draw. Paul had a ladder and a table to play with in coming up with these interesting positions. The organiser warned us, 'There's literally no telling what pose Paul will do!' In a tone of voice that suggested a degree of admiration, but also an overwhelming sense of terror. Paul lived up to the hype: over the next few hours he certainly did his best to acquaint us with as much of the space between his anus and scrotum as possible.

Ten minutes later I was sat with 20 other serious-looking artists (and Dave) staring at Paul, who was poised to disrobe. I was oddly nervous about life drawing. I had two main worries. Firstly, 'What if I get an erection?' And secondly, 'What if I get the giggles and can't stop? In front of all these proper artists?' Either eventuality would have been hugely embarrassing. And I'll tell you the truth, when Paul got his willy out I really got the giggles. Someone getting their willy out is always funny, isn't it? Unless they're on the night bus. When it's not funny. It's just sexy. But eventually I composed myself and got down to business. Drawing, it turns out, is really difficult. Hands and feet are especially tough, and faces are a nightmare. I mean, this was one of my early attempts:

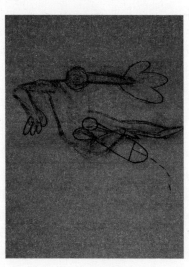

At the halfway stage there was a refreshments break. Paul (still naked) was doing the rounds cheerfully, chatting to everyone like a celebrity at a film premiere. He told me that he enjoys posing and that people often give him the drawings they've done of him. 'Do you keep them?' I said. He said he kept some of them and gives the rest to his mother. That would be a weird Christmas. Everyone sat around the tree opening their presents, laughing and sharing, and then it's mum's turn. 'Oooh what could this be? Let's see ... nice paper, I'll make sure I save that ... oh, there you are, Paul! Naked as the day you were born, hanging off a ladder ... circumcised I see? That's new! Thank you darling. I'll put it with the others...next to the plaster cast of your sister's tits.'

I was clearly rubbish at life drawing. But at least I knew that now. It struck me that we can never truly know our potential. We can only ever try a few things and so we never know if there is something out there that might be our calling. A strange thought suddenly occurred to me: 'I might be born to make jam!' I pondered. 'Maybe? I don't know. I've never tried. Maybe I can make jam so good it makes widows cum?' It was an unlikely scenario but I didn't want to die not knowing and so immediately my adventure took on an extra meaning. My journey was no longer just about learning how to be spontaneous, it was also about exploration of the self. My mind was agog with possibilities. 'Maybe I can throw a javelin into space?' I thought. 'Perhaps I am that good but I've never tried?' Imagine getting to ninety-years-old, seeing a javelin, throwing it, watching it soar into space and just thinking 'I'VE WASTED MY LIFE!' It didn't bear thinking about. Consequently I wanted to try everything; I vowed to find myself by doing more.

In that spirit, my next adventure was into the opaque world of taxidermy. If you've always dreamt of being a butcher but decided there weren't enough arts and crafts in it, then taxidermy is the hobby for you. Certain images came to mind when I thought about taxidermy: notably a stag's head riveted to the mahogany panelled living room of a country pile; or a stuffed weasel gawping creepily from the mantelpiece of a rural pub; or David Gest, who looks like he's had a stroke and then laminated it. I was apprehensive about taxidermy because I don't deal well with gore. I'm very squeamish. If someone suffers a bad injury on *Match of the Day* I can't watch the replay. It makes me feel sick. If I see blood in an episode of *Holby City* I stop masturbating. But it's not just blood and guts that make me squirm, it's also the thought of cutting up vermin. My worst fear is rats. I hate them. I'd rather be in a room with a bear than a rat, even if that bear was starving and furious and insisting I read their blog. So I had mixed feelings about taxidermy to say the least, but I was a slave to the Groupon e-mail and so duty required that I man up and get on with it.

I found the workshop with difficulty, as usual. Eventually discovering the front door surreptitiously snuck away on a cobbled lane near Borough High Street. It was so well hidden that it seemed illicit. At the bottom of a rusted iron staircase lay a dusty basement room mired in the dank darkness of a 1950s honky-tonk. Inside this mysterious lair I found Mike. He was wearing a blue apron and had a coarse grey beard. When I walked in, he was hunched over a table sweeping dead butterflies into a bin-bag. As he carried out this macabre task he whistled unemotionally – like a serial killer Bill Oddie. Soon another man joined us. He was lanky and pale and had a ponytail. He wore a long leather black trench coat. His T-shirt had a skull on it. We all sat around the glass table in the middle of the room as if we were about to take part in a seance. Mike disappeared into a back room briefly. Making polite conversation, I asked my fellow workshopper, Seb, what had brought him here today. He said that his now former work colleagues had bought the workshop for him as a leaving gift. 'They said they thought it would be the perfect present for me,' he said. 'What made them think that?' I asked. 'I've always been obsessed with death,' he said. 'Right … that's … errr … cool?' I stuttered. 'What was your job out of interest, Seb?' 'I was a shop assistant at the Early Learning Centre,' he said.

Mike returned clutching a large transparent polythene bag. He then emptied a variety of frozen corpses onto the work surface. Fifteen icy carcasses glistened as Mike arranged them into species. 'Right, we've got hamsters, gerbils, guinea pigs, or African rats. What do you want?' My fellow student began picking them up and comparing them as if sizing up a supermarket avocado. 'The gerbil is the big one, right?' said Seb. 'I think I'll have one of those because I want something large enough to go on top of the tree at Christmas.' I stared at him in disbelief but Mike nodded as if this was a great idea. Seb then dipped into his rucksack and pulled out an enormous plastic sparkly fairy. 'I'm going to remove the wings and the halo and make the gerbil wear them.' Again Mike nodded sagely. 'I tried to find a Barbie so I could rip out her eyes but everyone had sold out.' I was starting to see why Seb might have lost his job at the Early Learning Centre.

I chose a hamster. 'I had a hamster when I was a kid,' said Seb sounding human for the first time. 'But I dropped a sofa on it by accident and it died.' Nope, straight back to psycho again. The first stage in the taxidermy process was defrosting the animal's stomach, warming it with the palm of my hand. Then we made our first incision. I looked at my artillery of surgical instruments and chose a scalpel, making a cut of about three inches along the hamster's midriff. 'Don't go too deep,' warned Mike, 'you want to avoid bursting its stomach and intestines. Unless you're into that?' Not really Mike, no. We then spent 40 minutes on the gruesome task of removing the skin from the meat of the animal. 'Anyone else feeling hungry?' asked Seb.

Mike said most of the animals he uses for taxidermy have died in pet shops. Presumably of natural causes, or in fights, or in suicide pacts. Sometimes pest controllers might ring up and say: 'Hi mate, we've got 200 squirrels in our freezer, do you fancy them?' And Mike would say, 'No, I don't fancy them, but I will take them off your hands for taxidermy.' But animals are never bred exclusively for taxidermy. 'Could I bring my own animal to stuff?' asked Seb. 'What? Like a pet?' I said. 'Yeah maybe … or just animals I've … you know … found?' I stared back at Seb dumbfounded. What the hell did he have in his freezer? 'People ring up the whole time asking if they can stuff their pets,' piped up Mike. 'Often before they've even died yet.' That seems harsh don't you think? Looking at your beloved family dog walking around the garden, with hope and kindness in its eyes, and just thinking 'Rover would look *great* on the dining room wall'.

Having skinned my hamster it was time to start work on the body. You make the frame by wrapping wood wool around a piece of wire until it roughly resembles the shape of the animal you've just dissected. You then put the skin back over the top of it and sew everything shut. The last thing you add are some plastic eyes, which you insert through the mouth and push into the empty sockets. Seb chose to put large red eyes into his gerbil, so it looked possessed. He also soon gave up attempting to make it look like a festive fairy and instead pulled an Action Man doll from his rucksack. Ten minutes later the gerbil had an AK-47 in his hands. It looked terrifying. 'I'm going to call it Joseph Gerbils,' said Seb. 'What? As in Joseph Goebbels? The

Nazi?' I said. 'Obviously,' snickered Seb, looking at Mike. Both of them rolled their eyes. 'Happy Christmas, Seb,' I said.

Despite having accidentally amputated two of his limbs, I was proud of how my hamster had turned out. Later, in the pub, I told Dave to shut his eyes and presented my beautiful handiwork on the table in front of him. 'You can open your eyes now, Dave,' I said. Dave screamed and jumped off his bar stool. 'What the hell have you done to that ferret?' He said. 'It's a hamster, Dave.' 'It's a fucking monstrosity, that's what it is. Get it out of my sight.' I put the poor sod back into my bag as Dave climbed back on his stool. A waitress came over and dumped a steaming plate of steak and chips in front of him. 'That's really put me off my food that has,' said Dave whilst cramming eight chips into his slobbering gob. 'I thought I did a really good job for a beginner,' I said, genuinely wounded. 'You shouldn't do that to animals, it's cruel,' said Dave, now tucking into his steak like the greedy hypocrite he is. 'I need to think of a name for him,' I said. 'He looks like Noel Edmonds,' shot back Dave, gravy squirting from his mouth. And thus my pride and joy was christened.

Whatever Dave thought about my hamster, he couldn't deny that I had something to talk about at last. Before I'd begun this whole adventure, every story I'd tell about myself was from the distant past. My personality had first coalesced and then disintegrated; in social situations I behaved from memory, devoid of new experience to sow in the conversational fields. I was a fallow human. But things were different now. I was suddenly king of the anecdote and I liked it. If only Jen could see me now! Proud of my progress, I resolved to continue to bury myself under an avalanche of Groupons. My parents were growing impatient though. It was now late December 2013. I was still living in their house and they were openly talking about how much money they could make if they rented out my room on Airbnb. I was the one thing standing between them and a bungalow in Mallorca. But I couldn't afford to move out, not with my new lifestyle.

Christmas was looming but I got back on the Groupon treadmill for one final fling before the traditional Yuletide hiatus. On a cold Saturday morning in very late December I took part in the Outdoor Swimming Society's December Dip. It was held at Parliament Hill Lido near Hampstead Heath. The task was simple: swim two lengths of the pool in water measured at four degrees centigrade. To put that into context, the North Sea comes in at around nine degrees, and Piers Morgan's heart at seven degrees. But despite the icy cold water I wanted to take on this challenge for what it symbolised. Diving into discomfort seemed a metaphor for my entire project, and this experience would prove I could and would take the plunge.

The preliminary e-mail I'd received included a liability disclaimer form, which is never a good sign. It warned that there was a reasonable chance of croaking it in the pool, and that we would only be allowed in if, in the event of our death, we promised not to moan about it. I really didn't want to die in the pool. Obviously I didn't want to die full stop, but passing away in a swimming baths would be a very embarrassing way to go. It would be so anticlimactic – literally a damp squib. I don't want to die in any way that would make someone laugh when they heard. I don't want an old school friend to shuffle up to my grieving mother at my funeral, ask how I perished, and be told 'He went swimming, and, well … he got a bit cold'. I want to die doing something magnificent. Because your death goes a long way to deciding your legacy, it creates your myth. The elderly shouldn't wait for the inevitable march of time to claim them; when they hit seventy they should get into heroin or start wrestling bears. Really go out with a bang. Write an unforgettable epitaph for their gravestone: '*Sonia Brecknock, 1917-2015. She lived as she died: punching a bear in the dick*'.

Outdoor swimming is a growing hobby in the UK, with enough fans to support a monthly magazine. This month's edition included a profile on a swimmer genuinely called Helen Dolphin. What a beautiful example of nominative determinism. Helen Dolphin has read her name and thought: yes, I think it will be swimming for me. Good luck to her. I wish her and her fiancé, Tony Gigolo, all the best for the future. I'm a big swimming fan myself. In fact, I only joined my gym because they have a pool. I'm not popular though because I always forget my trunks. (Not deliberately, I'm just forgetful.) So I end up going swimming in my pants. A lot of people think it's weird going swimming in your pants, but to me it's the most logical thing in the world. You go swimming in your trunks because it hides your penis basically. But you could use anything: you could use a coconut, you could use a strawberry. I love going for a swim in my pants because it adds a sense of jeopardy to every swim. And when you get out of the pool, you get to see what your penis would look like if it were vacuum-packed.

Poolside at the Lido the atmosphere was a maelstrom of Britishness. A brass band banged out festive favourites, mince pies were scoffed, and a competition was held to find 'The Best Dressed Dipper'. An old lady dressed as Mr T took the crown – but the police forced her to give it back. The real winner was a woman with a huge Loch Ness monster tethered to her back. And she deserved her title: it was massive. But after these jolly pleasantries it was now finally time to throw ourselves into the drink. I was really pumped up. I am ridiculously competitive when I swim. This is how competitive I am in the pool: I race other swimmers even though they're not aware that I'm racing them. I looked out across the width of the pool and spotted this guy about two-thirds of the way up. I thought, 'I'm going to take this loser.' And I absolutely bolted it and I beat him, celebrating like I'd won Olympic gold. Because that was a big deal, you know? Because he had a massive head start. And also he was wearing armbands.

The water was freezing. As soon as I jumped in all breath was exorcised from my body through a series of embarrassingly loud guttural groans. I sounded like a hippo orgasming. Soon my whole body felt paralysed by the icy anaesthetic that now gripped it, but I thrashed my way to the end as quickly as I could. The Best Dressed Dipper had to be rescued by lifeguards after she began to drown. Her feather-light, papier-mâché Loch Ness Monster turning into a stone-heavy anchor on contact with the water. When I clambered back ashore every limb felt wooden and numb. But as the blood flow returned, I began to feel invincible. My skin glowed. I felt fresh and powerful and new. I was a roar made flesh. And as I sat on the bus on the way home I reflected that how I felt physically after my swim, mirrored how I now felt emotionally from My Groupon Adventure as a whole. Mentally I felt like I'd discovered new gears. Because these last couple of months I'd remembered how to play again. I had rediscovered my *joie de vivre*.

Much to Dave's chagrin I was bang on target too. I'd been going just over a month and a half and had completed six Groupons. (One a week plus his dog yoga gift.) This meant he was just 46 Groupons away from losing his beloved CD collection. I was proud of my progress. But not everyone was as enthusiastic about My Groupon Adventure. Some people labelled my project 'childish' or 'silly'. Well, if what I was doing was childish then I didn't want to grow up. Growing up so often seems to involve a cynical resignation to the state of the world and with it a sneering and amused condescension to anyone who rebels against it. To aspire for more is seen as pitifully naive. The irony is that this desperation to fit into such a prescriptive idea of what it is to be an adult, could not be more adolescent. I was proud to no longer be part of this Faustian pact with mediocrity. For me it came down to one crucial question: what do you think life is *for*? The stakes were that high. I wanted a life full of emotional juice. And I was getting there. I had given myself permission to experiment, to look silly, to pursue seemingly meaningless digressions. And in doing so I had become a lot happier. Suddenly I wished there were 48 hours in a day, 14 days in a week, and 1,000 days in a year. But little did I know that things were about to get much more complicated.

Chapter Four

Christmas time was not easy. Inevitably I missed Jen like never before and the holiday interlude of Groupons meant I had too much time to dwell on it. I also wasn't getting on with my parents. My mum and I row a lot at the best of times, but this Christmas things had hit an all-time low. This was mainly down to her furious response to my Christmas present. (Noel Edmonds was not a popular gift. And neither was my drawing of Paul.) Also, on Christmas Eve, my eldest cousin had announced he was to marry his girlfriend at the end of August. Consequently, since then, it was all my mum had banged on about. ('He's the same age as you and he's got a fiancée, a great job, and a mortgage. What have you got? Psoriasis.') This morning had brought an especially thick barrage, even by her standards though. My father and I tried to ignore her as best we could: him by doing the crossword, me by playing 'Angry Birds'. 'No phones at the table, Max!' said Mum, putting some toast on Dad's plate. 'Oh for God's sake. I'm 26!' I said. 'Exactly,' she replied, 'isn't it time you moved out? This is our house, our rules.'

'Eight across. "Weak, worthy of shame", said Dad. 'No idea,' said Mum, pouring more orange juice into my glass. 'It's good for your skin, love. You're flaking again, Max. You'll never find a girlfriend if you've got a face like an Eccles cake.' I rolled my eyes. 'You're obsessed, Mum!' 'I'm not obsessed. It's just …

well it's been three months now. I worry about you, darling. Three months turns into three years, three years turns into 10 years, and before you know it you're murdering prostitutes.' 'Pathetic,' said Dad. 'What?' I snapped. '"Weak, worthy of shame": pathetic. I'm almost finished. Darling ... nine down, "Partial to fantasies and self-deceit". Mum was now wetting down my hair with her spit. 'Oh, I'm no good at these, I'm afraid, darling. Max, your cousin called last night. He wants to know if you'll need a plus one for the wedding?' 'Yes. Definitely,' I said with maximum conviction. 'Delusional!' said Dad. 'I've finished the bugger!' The doorbell rang and I sprinted out of the kitchen. 'Where are you going, darling?' asked Mum. 'Oh ... me and Dave are going on a brewery tour,' I said. 'Have a nice time! If you get lucky tonight, text me and I'll hide your self-help books.'

On the tube I told Dave about my cousin's announcement. 'I remember my dad saying once, that marriage was like serving a life sentence in the worst prison on earth,' said Dave morosely. 'I remember that,' I said, 'it ruined your sister's wedding.' Dave nodded. 'And my brother's. Speeches aren't his forte, to be fair,' he said. 'This is really bad news, Dave. This is not good at all.' 'Why? It will be a fun do. Maybe I could DJ?' 'You're not DJ'ing, Dave.' 'Let's not rule it out as this stage.' 'You're not DJ'ing, Dave.' 'Never say never.' I should have felt pleased for my cousin, but I didn't. Because suddenly I had a deadline to win Jen back. I *had* to have a 'plus one' for my cousin's wedding. If I didn't I'd never hear the end of it. Mum would have a field day. Things now suddenly felt quite urgent.

We were en route to a tour of one of East London's many 'micro-breweries', hand-making craft lagers for the now burgeoning market. For readers not familiar with what East London is like these days, let me explain. It's no longer the preserve of cockneys, dancing a jig around the piano, eating pie and eels out of their hats. Now it's been trendified. It's like an urban Mordor, but instead of orcs it's populated exclusively by house DJs dressed like fourteenth century peasants. The brewery was crammed into a refurbished railway arch in Bethnal Green. One of four breweries on this street alone, there were also lots of quirky cocktail bars serving incandescent potions in jam jars and artisan Scotch eggs that cost more than a house in Middlesbrough. Next door was a pretentious coffee shop. We went in for a quick caffeine boost. You've probably been to one of these places: the tables are recycled doors, the chairs are recycled oil drums, and the staff are recycled actors. It takes them half an hour to make you a latte because the coffee is filtered through the digestive system of an owl. So far, so clichéd. We didn't have a look at the other hip boutiques occupying the remaining arches, but I imagine there was some sort of 'urban farm', a pop-up porridge restaurant, and someone dressed like Napoleon selling gluten-free vintage top hats.

Dave and I walked into the brewery, greeted by a forest of fat tubes and a stooping family of metallic silos. We found a naked wooden staircase and climbed it. At the summit was an open-plan bar area. Hunched behind the bar lurked a man with a dyed white beard. Yet another tick in the hipster box. 'You must be here for a tour? I'm Mark,' he laboured in rich Scottish tones. 'I must apologise if I'm sluggish today, I'm really hung-over. It was quite a big night last night.' 'No worries,' I said. 'Were you drinking here?' 'Aye,' he said. 'You could say you organised a piss-up in a brewery!' I quipped, before high fiving myself until my wrists snapped. Mark pulled three beers, taking one for himself. 'Hair of the dog!' he said, burgundy blood vessels webbing his face.

We began the tour, smelling a jar of the malty barley. Two

other staff members emerged from nowhere, both of them also drinking. It was two o'clock in the afternoon and everyone was getting battered. Mark showed us the brewing process and told us that his team bottle and label all the beers by hand. That's part of the joy of craft beer: the ridiculous names. You might have a swig of *Uncle Pete's Naughty Finger*, or a mouthful of *Gimme Hope Jo'Anna*. Also craft beer actually tastes of something. It's more expensive than mainstream lager, but I don't mind shelling out for superior flavour. Dave disagreed. 'I don't drink for enjoyment, I drink to forget,' he said, morbidly. Then I bought him some crisps and he soon cheered up. It turned out Dave wasn't depressed at all: he just hadn't eaten lunch.

I don't want to make any flippant generalisations about alcohol, but let's face it: alcohol is brilliant and life is worthless without it. I yearn for excitement, but when you're sober you're never surprised. I've never been on a dry night out and then been asked the next morning, 'Do you remember last night Max? When you arm wrestled that lesbian?' Those who think they have squeezed every drop of adventure from life have never gone online shopping when they're drunk. I go boozing, get back at three o'clock in the morning, go on eBay. Two weeks later some bloke from DHL turns up asking me to sign for a life-size edible Hitler. Alcohol also has some unheralded, but glorious, side effects. For example, I have no sense of direction normally. Zero radar. I'll contrive a way to get lost on the most simple of journeys. But if I'm drunk I can find my way home from anywhere in the world. It's like I'm a human TomTom. After a skinful, you could drop me into the middle of the Arctic tundra and I'd be back home by dawn. Not only that, but I can also run faster and with a stamina a sober me could only dream of. Normally I get tired when brushing my teeth, but eight pints turns me into Paula Radcliffe. By which I mean: I have the endurance to run a marathon and the propensity to defecate in the street.

Of course drinking is very bad for you. But so what? We fetishise health now. People want to live forever. I read in the paper that scientists are giving the elderly bionic bodies to help them live longer and longer. That's not progress, is it? I don't want my lovely dear old gran to be made into a robot! I mean, the last thing you want to do to a racist is make them indestructible. But when you're lying on your deathbed, the dewy gaze of your loved ones clinging to you like mooring lines, your ship about to leave this mortal port – you won't wish that you'd eaten more hummus. You'll mourn the people you wish you'd told you loved; the lakes you didn't swim in at midnight; the dogs you could have shaved. And all these are facilitated by alcohol, that moreish steroid of joy. So I'm proud to tell you that after the brewery tour, Mark, Dave and I got absolutely hammered on *Gandhi's Tears*.

The next morning, hung-over and queasy, I woke up and checked my e-mail. Within seconds it had become clear that I'd made another purchase. No, I hadn't forked out for a chocolate Kim Jong-un. I was in possession of a shiny new Groupon for something called a 'Gong Bath'. That's what it said. *Gong Bath*. It sounded like a character from a bad Hollywood B-movie, not a thing that you could actually *do*. Yes, Gong Bath would have a tan and a mullet and wear a white sports jacket. He'd say things like, 'Hi, I'm Gong Bath. Now park my speedboat whilst I make love to your wife.' I had no idea what the hell it was, but my new mission was to say 'yes' and possibly regret it later, rather than say 'no' and definitely miss an opportunity. And so that wet Sunday afternoon I set off on another voyage. 'What you up to now?' asked Dad, as I put on my coat. 'Oh I'm just going for a Gong Bath,' I said. 'Who is this Gong fellow?' asked Mum. 'And why are you having a bath with him?' 'It's not an actual bath, Mum,' I said. 'You need a girlfriend,' said Dad, shaking his head and returning to his *Sunday Times*. 'You might meet someone there?' said Mum hopefully. 'Yeah,' said Dad, 'it could be "Girls Gong Wild"'. Mum practically wet herself.

The venue was in a community centre near Waterloo station. I followed the laminated signs down a long corridor, deeper and deeper into the guts of the building, eventually coming to a set of double doors. I took a deep breath and stepped through, emerging into a dark room hot with incense. I could hear pan pipes. Immediately I was enveloped in a hug from a hairy bloke called Otto. He was bearded, with long hair and dressed in Eastern robes – so he looked somewhere between Peter Sutcliffe and Peter Pan. I'm not a good hugger at the best of times, especially when ambushed. I find it really awkward. If you get a hug from me it must be because someone you love has literally just died. In all other circumstances a handshake will suffice. So as Otto loomed I just stood there with my hands by my sides, all stiff and weird. Otto was incredibly enthusiastic though, grasping my reluctant torso like a teddy bear cuddling a breadstick. With Otto straddling me, I looked out into the gloom. A variety of different gongs had been arranged in the middle of the room, enormous metallic plates with their mallets hanging next to them portentously. Around the perimeter of the gongs lay yoga mats. I was the last one to arrive and everyone else had already taken their position spreadeagled on the floor, eyes shut, drinking in the mystical music. Otto gestured to a vacant mat.

'OK, we're going to start now,' said Otto in a Germanic whisper, his soft speech tiptoeing into my ears. 'This will take about an hour. All I ask you to do is to surrender to the gong. Don't fight it, don't resist it. Give in to the gong. If you submit to the gong, insight will be revealed, I promise.' I inwardly baulked at this idea. Surely it was a ludicrous notion: could the sound of a gong really change my life? He began to play, sensuously massaging a gong with his mallet. Suddenly I could feel vibrations shake through my body. It felt like being tickled from the inside. Then I started to trip, spiralling deep into hallucination. It was genuinely incredible: it was as if I was on acid. I couldn't tell you what I hallucinated, though. It's like when you awake from a dream: you know you've had one, but you can neither remember nor explain it. Then I suddenly came round, blurting out a bizarre noise, and flapping my arms in panic, accidentally slapping the woman next to me in the face. Luckily she didn't seem to notice.

Otto danced from gong to gong, hairy and agile, like a mountain goat. He would start with soft tones before taking us up to a dramatic crescendo. Following my sleepy spasm I regained my composure and immersed myself again. Otto had shifted from gongs and was now playing some delicate bells. The bells grew louder and louder until I felt surrounded. Fearful, I opened my eyes to see Otto bent over me, waving the bells inches from my face. He was now topless for some reason. He hopped around the room giving everyone the same treatment, before repeating it with a variety of increasingly bizarre instruments: triangle, wobbleboard, tin whistle.

The session came to a close and Otto instructed us to sit up on our mats, facing each other. He said it was time for discussion and that we should listen to each other with our hearts and without judgement. 'Does anyone want to say anything?' asked Otto softly. An America girl with dreadlocks spoke up in an LA drawl, '*Oh My Goooooddddddd such a trip*'. Otto nodded serenely. 'Yeah, but where does it come from, Otto? What's the science?' I asked. 'You've experienced a feeling,' he said, 'don't intellectualise it.' 'Yeah, but is there any evidence it actually works?' Otto looked saddened by my question. 'The gongs change the frequencies of your brain waves to "alpha". Alpha brain waves are linked to daydreaming, creativity and associative thinking. They have a similar effect to psychedelic drugs like LSD. But there's no need to question it, just accept the wisdom it reveals to you.'

An English girl in a denim jumpsuit, wearing enormous glasses with no glass in them, now took the baton. I'd seen her outside the community centre earlier, eating dried crickets from a knitted pouch. 'I just want to say that this was a really transformational experience for me.' Everyone was nodding now. 'I arrived here in quite a bad place, I've been having problems standing up to my mother and I felt like I had this blockage in my throat. But the gongs really smashed it to tiny bits and I feel like I can breathe again. So what I took away from today was a message that I really need to speak up and tell my own personal truth.' This got a round of applause.

'Anyone else want to say anything?' asked Otto. 'I do,' said the woman directly to my left. 'Great,' said Otto. 'I just want to say that I felt there was some hostility in the room today,' she said. 'Please continue,' says Otto pressing his hand to his heart, 'This is a safe space. What do you mean by hostility?' 'Well, the gentleman on my right punched me in the face.' 'OH COME ON!' I said. 'Do you deny this, Max?' said Otto. 'I completely and utterly deny it,' I said, 'I did not punch you in the face!' 'Yes you did!' said the woman pointing at a fresh blue bruise.' 'No, I did not!' I said, 'I *slapped* you in the face. Big difference.' 'You slapped this woman in the face?' said Otto, concerned. 'It was an accident! I woke up from a dream and panicked. I think I thought she was a troll or something.' I tried to start another round of applause but this time no one joined in. Otto then asked me to leave.

The next morning I reflected on my experience at the Gong Bath and felt embarrassed. Not because I'd accidentally punched a young woman in the face. (I'd done it before and I'll probably do it again.) It was clear I still had a long way to go. If I was going to make the most of My Groupon Adventure, then I needed to be more open-minded. Especially considering what I was about to do next: I was going to be neck deep in a whole new level of weirdness.

Chapter Five

'You're not leaving this house until you've tidied your room.' Mum was on the warpath yet again. 'Actually Mum, I realised at the Gong Bath that sometimes you really stifle me and it's about time I spoke up and told my personal truth,' I said. 'Don't be such a wanker,' she said. So I tidied my room. Confrontation has never been my strong point, but this morning I was off to a place where that wouldn't be a problem. I was about to spend four days at a silence retreat. How do you think you'd cope? Four days of total hush without so much as a muttered 'thank you' or a cursory 'good morning'? This was this challenge that awaited me as my taxi drew up outside Gaia House. A sanctuary anchored in the oscillating green sea of Exmoor.

I was here because I was stressed out. My mind a turbid, tumbling river; a chain gang of thought; all commas, no full stops. Waterboarded with worry, I was living permanently in the future: whipped and harangued by my phone, enslaved by e-mail, unable to concentrate on anything for more than a minute. I'd become incapable of reading. At the end of every paragraph I'd need a pit stop. I could no longer enjoy books, my intellectual horizon was pure clickbait. I'd become a cat-obsessed, conspiracy theorist nymphomaniac. I needed to digitally detox. All that said, I was dreading these four days. I am not good at doing nothing. As Pascal once said, 'All humanity's problems stem from man's inability to sit quietly alone in a room.' And he wrote that in the seventeenth century – 300 years before *YouPorn*. Now, with the siren call of free online pornography, it's even harder.

Gaia House is run by Buddhists. I'd always been curious about Buddhism. I like Buddhism because it's sort of God-lite. You get all the warmth of personal transcendence, of feeling part of something bigger than you, without having to believe in a bearded man in the sky who may or may not hate gay people. There is a head honcho (Buddha) but he isn't omniscient and omnipotent. He looks like Alan Sugar in a nappy. You don't fear him; you just want to tickle him. He's a kind of human Churchill dog. You can imagine having a nodding Buddha on your dashboard, cheering you up after you've just given a cyclist the finger. Buddha is not a god nor has he ever claimed to be. He was a man who simply taught the path to enlightenment from his own experience. His approach was basically: 'I did this and had a nice time, so why don't you give it a go yourself? PS Have you thought about trying wasabi peas?'

I had a number of prejudices about the retreat. For example, I assumed the coordinators would all be bonkers. They'd wander around barefoot, dressed in togas, permanently drinking nettle tea. There seems to be a definite correlation between esoteric spiritual beliefs and taste for weird teas. I'm not sure why. Perhaps alternative tea acts as a badge of membership? Just like having a beard tells people you're creative, and having a personalised number plate shows everyone you're a massive twat. If the coordinators weren't strange then I thought they'd be dodgy rip-off merchants. Because think about it: the silence retreat could be absolutely terrible but I wouldn't be able to complain.

Me: *'Excuse me, there's a dead body in the ...'*
Them: *'Ssshhhhh!'*

I got off the Mega Bus in Newton Abbot and took a cab to Gaia. The scenery was beautiful. Green hills undulated like waves of gazpacho. Stone bridges with crew cuts of moss straddled black waters eddying beneath them, pockmarked by rain. On arriving, I was shown round the old country house. On the wall of the dining area there was a sign, laminated and written in large red capitalised letters, which read: 'IN THE EVENT OF FIRE: STAY SILENT'. A coordinator told me that every morning at 7am we'd all have to do an hour of work. I'd been allocated gardening, which would involve 'heavy lifting'. In other words, I would be getting up at sunrise to do 60 minutes of unpaid manual labour. I must have been visibly unimpressed by this news because the facilitator trotted out that oldest of aphorisms, 'The early bird catches the worm'. This is clearly absolute drivel. Yes, worms come to the top of the earth when the dew of the early morning settles. If you are the first bird on the scene you will be clearly have a run on the worms. But opportunities don't work like worms, do they? They don't all float to the surface at sunrise; they appear at all times of day and almost always after breakfast. We've lived under the tyranny of this maxim for too long. A much better aphorism would be: 'The punctual owl catches the mouse', or 'Get up when you like, we're all just insignificant specks on a meaningless rock cascading towards certain death'.

The coordinator talked me through the schedule in more detail. Our hour of work would be followed by 10 hours of meditation, alternating between sitting and walking meditation. There would be three vegetarian meals served a day, he said. And as much herbal tea we could drink. Finally, I was shown to the dorm I'd be sharing with the other male guests. The retreat took in Valentine's Day, so I already expected the other participants would be mainly lonely, strange singletons like me.

And I was right. Fifteen pairs of dead eyes fixed on me as I entered the room. It was like some sort of rapists' awayday.

Most of my prejudices were proved to be exactly that. Yes, the place stank of incense; yes, there were a lot of wind chimes; and yes, when I first arrived a coordinator in a sarong did show me the outdoor compostable toilet whilst singing the virtues of having a crap as the cold wind blew through your pubic hair. But in general everyone was really normal. The first rule of silence club is that you don't talk in silence club. The second rule of silence club is that you don't talk in silence club. The third rule of silence club is please don't read, write or use any technology including your phone for the duration of your stay. So this was it. For the next four days I was totally unplugged and off-grid. I checked my e-mails one final time, deleting the latest missive from Groupon – '50% off entry to Britain's biggest cheese museum' was an opportunity I would have to spurn. I put my phone in my bag as the bell went to signal the start of silence. I would not say another word for over 90 hours.

Just after dawn the next morning all 20 of us were sat crossed-legged in the meditation hall. 'Whenever you get lost in thoughts, breath is waiting to welcome you back. Breath is your refuge,' said Kirsten, our German guru, who was the only person allowed to speak. In sitting meditation the idea is to focus on your breath and clear your mind of all thought. My first meditation was a disaster. My mind kept wandering from my breath – a restless moth pursuing a chaos of digressions. Such as ruminating on whether I could smell a fart (I could). Someone had let one off, which I suppose was unsurprising considering the diet here. The previous evening we'd had a lentil and chickpea stew, which stomach-wise is like pouring a bottle of Lucozade into a bucket of sherbet. I'd personally spent most of the night breaking wind to harrowing effect, unleashing a vortex of those really viscous farts that feel like your inner bum cheeks are being licked by a velvet tongue.

After a morning of meditation we retired for lunch. I was sat next to a man who spent 40 minutes staring at his hands. This was not deemed odd behaviour. Having eaten, I went to wash up my dishes at the sink area and saw this large handwritten note that one of the coordinators had posted on the wall:

'While washing the dishes one should only be washing the dishes. If while washing the dishes we think only of the cup of tea that awaits us, if we hurry to get the dishes out of the way as if they were a nuisance, then we are not alive during the time we are washing the dishes. If we can't wash the dishes then the chances are we won't be able to drink the tea either. While drinking the cup of tea we will be only thinking of other things, barely aware of the cup in our hands. Thus we are sucked into the future – and we are incapable of actually living one minute of life.'

A useful, profound and wise tip. And here's another: if you really want to enjoy the washing up, then run a soapy bath, take the dirty dishes in with you, turn on the shower, and pretend you're on a submarine that has been holed during battle. You're welcome.

In the walking meditation room stood a real human skeleton for us to look at and contemplate the impermanence of the universe. The skeleton was donated to Gaia House by a former retreatant who had presumably died of boredom. It's meant to be a *memento mori*, symbolising that everything in this life is in a state of flux. Thoughts, things, people: they come and they go. So we shouldn't get attached to anything. We need to bend around life like water, let life happen to us rather than resist it. The skeleton also carries another important message: life's too short. Which did beg the question: why was I spending Valentine's Day in silence staring at a skeleton?

With all the meditation I could feel myself changing. I was becoming more relaxed, happier and dare I say it, wiser. In fact, and this will irritate you, I'd go as far to say that I *found myself*. There, I said it. Feel free to shoot me in the face. I'm aware that 'finding yourself' is the sort of cliché babbled by gap year public school poverty tourists visiting Vietnam to gawp at orphanages, but hear me out. My reasoning is that there's a difference between 'thoughts' and 'insights'. Thoughts come at the end of a process, after a long chain of other thoughts. They often lead us nowhere useful because we get lost in them. Insights on the other hand are revealed to you fully formed, seemingly from your heart. Now obviously, biologically that's nonsense, but they do seem to come from somewhere different to your thoughts. These insights are revealed in moments of stillness when the dust has settled. These tend to be truer and more profound than mere thoughts. They contain the invisible, intangible essence of you. And by removing the mental static at this retreat I had allowed these insights to bubble to the surface.

So after three days I was ready to pack everything in and become a monk. Yes, I would spend the rest of my life meditating, eating gruel, and staring at my hands. I seriously began to doubt why I had become so obsessed with cramming more and more experiences into my life. Surely this was a zero-sum game if I wasn't actually ever fully in the moment actually *experiencing* them? I couldn't even wash up a mug for God's sake! So I told myself: enough is enough. I'll pack in My Groupon Adventure, buy a toga and go and live in Nepal for the rest of my life. Yeah, I'd write a new book instead, *Max in the Monastery*, and I'll spread love and peace round the world. After all, I was sure I could grow to like tofu. I mean, I was already halfway there: I liked toffee. And it's not like I was having a lot of sex anyway.

Plus bell-ringing looked like a good laugh. No, no, becoming a monk was the life for me. I was convinced.

That's how I felt at the end of day three. By the end of day four I wanted to set fire to myself. I was bored out of my mind. I'd realised that mindfulness is a useful skill but it's not a good lifestyle in itself. There is so much else to love about life. I could not withdraw from the world and deny myself all the brilliant things I'd experienced these past four months. Luckily there wasn't long left. We were coming to the end of our stay. Weirdly, despite not being able to talk to people, I had felt I got to know some of my fellow retreaters quite intimately. It's amazing how much rapport you can develop with facial expressions alone. I'd miss these guys. There was one chap, much older than me, who I'd got on with especially well. At lunch on the last day, for a treat, we were allowed to talk to each other for the first time. I was looking forward to chatting to my new friend. We sat opposite each other, said hello, then he start blathering on about something. After about two minutes I just thought, 'Shut the fuck up, mate. I preferred you when you were silent'. Grumpy Max was back. Let's face it, I could never be a monk. I'm not nice enough.

It was time to go. I bade farewell to the co-ordinators, leaving them to enjoy the compostable toilet in peace. In the taxi on the way back to Newton Abbot I turned on my phone for the first time in almost 100 hours, awaiting the flood of e-mails, a blizzard of texts, a monsoon of tweets. There was nothing – save for a few e-mails from Groupon and a text asking me if I'd thought about claiming for PPI. I wasn't anywhere near as popular as I'd thought. I clambered back onto the Mega Bus and dwelt on what I'd learnt at Gaia. I'd learnt one of the biggest lessons of My Groupon Adventures so far. Namely that there are a million ways to live a life. There are so many different beliefs, so many different motivations, and there's room for everyone. We as individuals just have to find the one that suits us best and then have the courage to stand by it. I was galvanised by this fresh conviction to keep searching, to keep on trying new things. A few hours into my journey my phone finally buzzed again with another text. 'Your cousin wants to know if you want lamb or salmon at the wedding? Also, I assume there's no plus one?' It was from my mum. I sighed. This was a depressing reminder of what I was going back to. But luckily for me a big change lay around the corner.

Chapter Six

I hadn't heard from Jen for a while. Which was a shame because if we went for a coffee now I knew I would absolutely blow her socks off. Five minutes with me and she'd be begging me to take her back. After all, I'd *found myself.* Over these past months, through the power of adventure, I had been transformed. I was desperate to prove to her that I was a different, better, more exciting man. I was convinced she would fall in love with me again. If only I could get her to reply to one of my texts. So in one sense things were going brilliantly: I was 12 weeks into my 52-week odyssey and still going strong. I had genuinely become more spontaneous. But in another sense things were getting out of hand. I was spending almost all my spare time on Groupon deals, ignoring my friends. So I decided to organise a night out to catch up with all the people I'd been neglecting. After all, I had so much to tell them! And I wanted it to be a Groupon so I could introduce them to the magic.

I took them to the dogs in Wimbledon for an evening of greyhound racing. Essentially you watch some dogs chase a fake hare around a track for about three hours and lose a fortune to bookmakers. But it's loads of fun. I actually prefer dog racing to horse racing because it looks endearingly amateur. It genuinely looked like a bunch of dodgy cockney men had just turned up with a dog they'd stolen. Nobody had a clue what was going on, the stadium was a dump, the food was disgusting: it was brilliant. Sport has got too professional. There's no human element in it anymore. It's all so high-tech and big-budget. The athletes are like robots now. I can't relate to them. I want to watch people like me: real, flawed idiots. I tell you what I want to watch, I want to watch some fat men run around a pub car park, chasing some crisps. Put that on the TV. Sky Sports should be chomping at the bit.

The reason why dog racing is fun is that nobody has the foggiest idea about who's going to win. It appears almost random. So you just go on the name of the dog.

'I'm putting a tenner on "Hitler's Boyfriend", what about you, Dave?'

'I've got twenty quid each way on "I Can't Believe It's Not Horse."'

But just as drugs have been an issue in professional sport, doping is also apparently a big problem in greyhound racing. To try and combat the issue, attempts are made by the authorities to get urine samples from all the dogs who have taken part in the race. God knows how you get a urine sample from a pooch. It's not like you can give a dog a beaker and direct it to a cubicle. Do you disguise yourself as a tree and just wait, hoping to catch whatever you can in a bucket? Either that or you could just take it to doga, I suppose, and then just sponge it off the mats. A greyhound's career lasts between four and six years. But what do the greyhounds do after they retire? I assume some of them become pundits. Apparently one in four are adopted as pets, and the rest are destroyed. That's how they talk about killing a dog. Not 'put down', not 'euthanized', no – *destroyed*. That's terrible! Imagine if we talked about a human being like that. There would be outrage.

'Where's Auntie Anne this Christmas?'

'Oh. Sad news, actually. Auntie Anne got quite ill, so she took herself off to Switzerland and she was destroyed.'
'OH MY GOD! What was it? Lethal injection?'
'No. Controlled explosion.'

'Destroyed' is a strange word to use. It does beg the question, how exactly are they getting rid of these dogs? Blowing them up with missiles? Dropping them out of planes? If only my old pal Seb knew that there were this many dogs going spare. He'd have stuffed an entire army's worth by now. But despite this morbid backdrop, we had a brilliant time at the greyhounds. And I was proud to show off my new sociable self. Then the following week, at a Groupon Murder Mystery party, something strange happened. I randomly met some old university pals I'd lost touch with during my wilderness years. Over some drinks in the bar afterwards, Philippa and Hope told me that they had a spare room in their flat that needed filling and asked if I might be interested in taking it. It was an emergency, they said. They wouldn't ask me unless they were absolutely desperate. And they couldn't have been clearer about that, but someone had let them down and I'd really be helping them out. I said I'd mull it over. It was a big decision and I said I wanted to take the maximum possible time to think it through.

At six o'clock the next morning I woke my parents up and told them that I was leaving. They both burst into tears. I didn't know what to say. I felt absolutely terrible for making them feel so sad. I'd broken their hearts. They hugged each other tightly, dabbed their eyes with hankies, and my mother finally composed herself enough to speak. 'This is the happiest I've felt since you gave up the clarinet!' she said. 'Yes!' said Dad, 'We can finally rent out your room … I mean we'll have to have it fumigated first, obviously … but this is great news! Spain here we come!' Mum and Dad then sang *Livin' La Vida Loca* to each other whilst dancing around the kitchen. My room was listed on Airbnb by midday and I'd moved out by teatime. I'd finally left home! And it was all because of Groupon.

That evening I unpacked my bags and settled into my new bedroom. There was a knock on the door and Philippa walked in. 'Just thought I'd pop my head in to see how you're getting on. What the hell is that?' she said, pointing at the wall. 'Oh it's a photo of some rocks,' I said. 'God, it's not from Ikea, is it?' 'Errr … no?' 'It is though, isn't it?' 'Yes.' 'Oh Christ, you're not *that guy* are you? What have you got planned for the other wall? An Audrey Hepburn poster?' I laughed nervously. 'I don't want to be a dick about it, but the landlord doesn't let us put stuff on the walls, so can you take it down?' she continued. 'Sure,' I said. I'd just moved in and I didn't want to upset the apple cart. Philippa left and I turned on my laptop to check my e-mail. Inevitably there was one from Groupon. I looked at the subject line, 'Could you be the UK's next great street artist?' And I thought, 'Yes, actually. I think I can.' For the first time in years I felt self-confident. I was plump with chutzpah. So I booked a class for the very next day. After all, if I wouldn't need to put art on the wall if the entire world was my canvas.

I awoke the next morning feeling nervous: I would be totally out of my depth. I thought it would be me and 12 *yoofs* in hoodies. We'd be taught by a gang leader and part-time grime MC called 'Death Row' (or something). We'd all meet underneath a railway bridge somewhere awful and do a weird handshake that I wouldn't understand, inject ketamine into our eyes, and then gallivant around London moving exclusively using parkour. As it turned out, the workshop was in an art gallery in Ladbroke Grove, wedged in between a boulangerie and a Pilates centre. I felt at home. I arrived at midday but everything was locked.

So I rang the bell and a scrawny Scottish guy answered the door in just his Y-fronts. 'What time is it?' he asked, bleary-eyed. That was the first thing he said. There wasn't even a perfunctory 'Hello'. Just straight into a demand. In a Scottish accent so viscously deep that he actually sounded Nigerian. So I'm looking at this borderline transparent man stood in front of me and I'm thinking: 'Is this some sort of weird test? Is it a gang-style initiation? Maybe there's a special password?' So I think on my feet and zing straight back, 'According to my watch it's graffiti o'clock!' He stares at me like I've just broken into his house on Christmas Day and set fire to his nan. And then he reluctantly lets me in. Before staggering upstairs to put some trousers on.

I waited uneasily in the gallery and checked out the exhibits. Street art is meant to be 'dangerous'; it's meant to smash the system. But my mum's got a Banksy print in her kitchen. She bought it in John Lewis. Art can't be dangerous if it's in a category of things labelled 'stuff my mum likes'. It's on the same list as Michael Bublé, Herbal Essences and Kettle Chips. The only system my mum's brought down is the Ticketmaster booking system when she accidentally bought 2,000 tickets to *Loose Women Live*. Eight other wannabes joined me in the studio to be addressed by the pale Scottish man. He said that his street alias was Blitz ('because I keep dropping truth bombs'), and he insisted that we should all call him that throughout.

The basis for street art is initially drawing an image onto some paper and then cutting it out to create a stencil, which you use to spray-paint your final piece. Jay said the stencils are crucial because they allow you to be quick. You can get the picture painted – on an underpass, say – and get out of there 'before the pigs turn up'. I asked Blitz what he was working on at the moment. He said he was going to spray a Hammersmith Council wheelie bin with an image of David Cameron eating a white-chocolate Magnum. Yeah! Take that *The Man*!

After this brief tutorial, we set to work on our canvases. But not before picking the truth shrapnel out of our eyes, obviously. Graffiti, it turns out, is lots of fun. Art was my favourite subject at school and it felt good to rediscover that passion. It seemed that Groupon was not just helping me to remake myself but also to remember myself too. Later that week was Dave's birthday. I hadn't seen him for a while, what with getting to know my new flatmates. He didn't mind though. Dave had spent most of that time travelling to Istanbul to see Vanilla Ice in concert. But I wanted to give him something special for his birthday, because, after all, my new spontaneous lifestyle was down to his intervention. So naturally I tapped into Groupon, and the following weekend we went fencing in North London. Dave was now inadvertently aiding and abetting the destruction of his own CD collection. And there was another subplot too, because this was to be my first sporting Groupon. To go with my spiritual, artistic and animal endeavours so far. I was a polymath: my spontaneity knew no bounds. Jen would not be able to deny I was changing.

The sport of fencing evolved in the eighteenth century when duels were used to settle judicial disputes and matters of honour. Between 1798 and the Civil War in 1861 the US Navy lost two-thirds more men to duelling than they did in actual combat at sea. The great uncle of the poet Lord Byron, William Byron, had a duel with his cousin and neighbour William Chatsworth for having the temerity to suggest that he had more birds in his garden. They had a sword fight in a local restaurant and Chatsworth died. Byron got off with a small fine. There's also another story about an Irishman who challenged a stranger to a duel because they'd suggested his claim to have seen a tree with anchovies growing on it, was clearly total horseshit. Having mortally wounded the naysayer, the Irishman then remembered that he meant to say *capers* and not anchovies. He went on to have a calamity-filled career with Domino's Pizza.

Duelling went into sharp decline after the First World War, but a version of it continued as fencing, only this time with weapons known as 'foils'. Foils are long pointy metallic sticks that you thrust at your opponent's torso to score points. So in the gym me, Dave and the rest of the crowd were taken through the basic techniques of the sport and then it was time for us to do battle on the strip. The instructor separated our group into pairs, trying to match us up with a partner of equal physical capacity. I learnt my opponent was to be a minute, adolescent Chinese girl called Lee. Poor old Lee had fainted at the start of the session due to illness, so I complacently donned my helmet preparing to give her the caning of a lifetime. For the next 20 minutes Lee absolutely schooled me. I don't think I scored a point. But she tired eventually and I scored a brave last-minute victory. 'Lee-sy peasy,'

I quipped, standing proudly over her exhausted and vanquished body. Lee pedantically disputed the result, claiming that points scored from kicks don't count. But the scoreboard never lies and that day the story was crystal clear: I had beaten that tiny, ill, Chinese child fair and square.

Chapter Seven

It was now springtime and just as the flowers had sprouted young buds, so had I. I was abloom with new interests. I had an adamantine glow: eyes bright with optimism, skin flush with ruddy determination. As the days grew longer so did my opportunity for adventure, the warm weather and freshly lavish plumage on the trees beckoning me outside. Back in the flat, I fired up my laptop and logged in to see what Groupon had in mind for me. I wanted to do something outdoors and quirky. I opened my e-mail and there, teetering at the top of 40 unopened messages, was a note from Groupon. 'Beekeeping day in West London' glistened the subject line. It was as if they could read my mind. Without a second's thought, I unfurled my credit card details and picked up the phone. 'Dave, we're going beekeeping, mate,' I said. I couldn't wait.

I always thought bees were wankers. Summer terrorists, suicide stingers; obsessed with sugar, like flying toddlers but with knives for an arse. When I heard that the world was facing a 'bee shortage', it sounded the same to me as if the world were facing a 'fart drought' or a 'dickhead famine'. Good riddance! I thought. We can do without honey, can't we? Who's it going to affect? Winnie the Pooh? He can do with laying off the stuff anyway. That's all he eats. He's probably diabetic by now. He's also very fat for a bear, and yellow, which is not healthy. He's got jaundice basically. So bees weren't top of my bucket list, but my relentless search for new experience drew me to the bastards and a small family home in Brentford. Where in the back garden were four hives containing almost 2,000 bees.

What comes to mind when you hear the words 'beekeeper'? You probably think of an old man with a beard living a hermit-like existence in rural Somerset; a vagabond who drinks milk straight from the udder and sleeps in a dilapidated caravan with only a goose for company. In short, you think of someone mental. But what struck me about this beekeeper was that she was totally ordinary. Lynn was a lovely lady living in a nice house with two children and a husband. Amateur beekeeping is much more popular than you'd think. Apparently there are 50 beekeepers in the Ealing area alone, so if we extrapolate that to the whole country that is an awful lot of beekeepers. Over honey cookies, I asked Lynn if the neighbours objected to her keeping a ton of bees. 'Oh yes, they're allergic to bees,' she said, as if that wasn't relevant. 'The bees do sometimes swarm, and obviously they get upset,' she added. 'Also there's a school down the road and they've been swarmed too, ruined their GCSE exams one year.' Well, bees will be bees.

Taking care of bees-ness with Dave and I, was the fattest woman in Europe. I don't know this for a fact. She wasn't wearing a medal and I haven't done a full survey. But she must have had the same BMI as an oil tanker. It felt dangerous to teach this lady how to rear her own bees. She'd basically have her own honey factory. That's like teaching a junkie how to grow his own heroin. It was time for us to don the bee suits. Dave and I put ours on without much hullaballoo. The lady needed help from all three of us. It was like pulling a condom over a cow. Having donned our protection, we went out to inspect the hives.

Lynn gave Dave a smoker, which is a set of bellows with a small fire burning within its belly. Beekeepers blow smoke into the hive before taking the lid off because it makes the bees think the hive's on fire so they gorge themselves on honey expecting a long fly, and end up eating so much that they can't be bothered to attack you. This was Dave's responsibility today. Unfortunately he obviously didn't do a thorough enough job because the bees were now swarming around the fat woman, probably because her blood was 80% Coca-Cola. She began to panic: waddling around in a circle, manically waving her hands in front of her face, gasping the word 'Help!' Lynn was calm as always: 'If you stop moving they'll relax,' she said with a shrug, 'There's no need to worry. You're wearing a protective suit!' No sooner had these words left her lips than a bee somehow broke into the fat woman's gauze helmet. All hell broke loose. 'I'm trapped!' yelped the woman, now literally punching herself in the face. Luckily Dave still had the smoker and so took the initiative, blowing smoke straight into the fat woman's eyes. This compounded matters. The fat woman was now screaming and sobbing. Lynn was at the end of her tether. She replaced the lid of the hive and the bees slowly returned. When the cloud of bees and the cloak of smoke had lifted we

returned indoors. 'What's the best way to treat a bee sting?' croaked the upset fat woman. 'Simple,' said Dave, 'you piss on it.' Dave reached for his flies as if ready to do the honours. 'No that's jellyfish, Dave,' I said, really regretting asking him to join me.

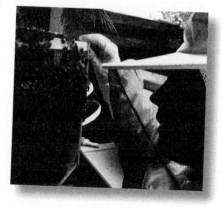

Our beekeeping experience concluded with honey tasting. You taste honey much like wine, taking in the aroma and then lingering on a mouthful, before making conceited and pretentious remarks about it. For example: 'I'm getting floral tones here and an aftertaste of GCSE exam papers.' Our host presented her award-winning honey from last year, which was delicious. 'At the competitions the honey is tasted blind,' she said. 'Well, they say blind people's other senses are more acute,' I ventured. 'No,' she said, sounding jaded, 'blind as in there are no labels on the jar.' The fat woman had jettisoned the wooden tasting sticks Lynn had provided and was now using a serving spoon to shovel the honey straight into her mouth. This was the final straw. Lynn shepherded us towards her front door, she'd had enough and I didn't blame her. Despite Dave's heroics, I'd had a brilliant day. The thousands of other lives we could be living haunt us all. The infinite number of forks in the road we might have taken. We've all fantasised about a parallel universe where we're a screenwriter in LA, or a deli-owner in Notting Hill, or a painter in Provence. Experiences like these feel like inhabiting the ghost of a life that died when we decided to do what we do now. It was a glorious escape, a seductive tease, and an amphetamine for My Groupon Adventure.

I was now 23 Groupons down: almost halfway to winning the bet with Dave. But my next deal wasn't just another step up my 52-rung Groupon ladder. I came to dispel a hoodoo from my childhood. Through the unlikely medium of a horse-riding lesson in Epping Forest. The stables were a short taxi ride from Loughton, almost at the very end of the Central Line. No one ever goes to the end of tube lines. Going beyond Leytonstone felt like entering a parallel underworld. Is it London still? Is it Essex? Who knows? It's amazing how terrible things get outside of London; even just a few feet away from it. Leaving London is like stepping through a portal to another time. Children are still eating Starburst, the Spice Girls are still at number one, and the air reeks of smouldering witches. Places outside the city just don't have any of the stuff I like. Before provincial readers get moody about my arrogant London-centrism, by doesn't have any of the stuff I like', I don't mean important stuff. Things that you have in glorious abundance like community or kindness. No, I mean the superficial and trivial stuff that actually makes life worth living. Like coffee shops or decent wi-fi and mini-marts that are open 24 hours a day. Basically, I don't want to live anywhere where I can't buy frozen lasagne at four o'clock in the morning. So you see I'm not being patronising (patronising means talking down to someone in a condescending manner). I don't think London is objectively better than where you live, just different in ways I prefer. Now chill out and have a pie.

In the cab I felt nervous. My parents will tell you a story about a six-year-old Max Dickins. We were at a fair during a summer holiday on the Isle of Wight. There were many amusements at this fete: one might go on the teacups or bob for apples. You could go into a tent and look at the Isle of Wight's only gay man. Or you could guess the weight of an asylum seeker to win a crab. There was also a bearded lady but she didn't do much business, because it was the Isle of Wight and so most of the women had facial hair anyway. One of the premier attractions at the fair was 'The Isle of Wight's longest horse', and you could pay a shilling to sit on it and have it walk about.

Being a prodigious brat, I insisted that this horse experience was absolutely essential. *'If I can tame this beast, mother, who knows what I might go on to achieve?'* I muttered through the candyfloss I was forcing into my moon face, like a megalomaniac Augustus Gloop. The horse was somewhat of a celebrity, and consequently my parents and I queued 45 minutes for my turn.

When I was finally beckoned to mount, I burst into tears and refused to get on. My fear of the stallion may strike rural readers as odiously wet. I understand they are ten-a-penny in the provinces; indeed, you probably have a horse for a mayor. But being a dyed-in-the-wool townie I'd never seen such a monster. My mother was sympathetic. But my father rolled his eyes and called me 'a pathetic waste of skin'. I've never forgotten.

So as I clambered out of the taxi, breathing in the manure rich air for the first time, I felt like a man on a mission. A farrier was at work in one stable, replacing the shoes of a pliant mare. The air smelt of solder and the plangent echo of hammer on metal drowned out the whinnying of the other steeds, whose lovably gormless faces hung out of their boxes. My group assembled to receive our equipment. It was me and seven black people. Which was a bit, well ... surprising. I'd always assumed horse riding was the preserve of white toffs: all double-barrelled surnames and Barbour jackets. I'd expected I'd be riding with a braying public school girl called something like Tabitha Celery-Quiche. I don't think I've ever seen a black guy on a horse in popular culture. Maybe I'm watching the wrong movies but I don't think it was racist of me to think it was a weird racial ratio. Anyway, I ventured some friendly small talk, 'So do you guys all know each other then?' I said like a fumbling buffoon. Everybody stared coldly back at me. 'No, why would we?' said one of them. 'Well ... no, no reason ... I just thought ... don't worry about it,' I said, before turning as red as my riding helmet.

Our first task was to groom the horse – so I added it on Facebook and sent him photos of my penis. All the horses were dead behind the eyes, like demoralised prostitutes. '"Waffles" loves being petted by you!' gushed a stable girl, in the manner of a deluded pimp. She then attached his bridle, compelling 'Waffles' to open his mouth revealing an enormous tongue, a tidal wave of peach-pink meat, lips like long fleshy levees and sharp dice for teeth. We dumped the saddle on and dragged 'Waffles' out into the yard. Other horses had also been assembled, huge battleships of cartilage and hair, and we each climbed on our ride. The stable girls led us around a field before chivvying the horses into a jog. Objectively, this wasn't very fast but I was absolutely terrified. Being on a horse is like being on a meat motorbike with no breaks and an ejector seat that might go off at any moment. I felt the tears welling in me again as catharsis became regression. I saw the ghost of my father leaning on the fence, shaking his head, mouthing the words 'pathetic waste of skin'. I resolved to tough it out.

A couple of hours later, cold and tired, we returned to the stables. I bade my horse goodbye and he neighed affectionately. With the others he does it for the sugar lumps but with me it was different. I actually think he would have done it for free. I actually think he liked me. In the lodge, a stable girl asked if I was hungry. 'Yes. I could eat a horse!' I said. Which was, admittedly, a poor choice of words. She hastily offered me a flapjack and, as I sat there chewing it, I reflected on the tiny victory today represented. I had slayed a dragon. This was yet another victorious excursion outside of my comfort zone. What's more, doing something that scared me had proven my commitment to this project. I was almost halfway to winning the bet. Next I would get a vote of confidence from the paranormal world.

Chapter Eight

Things were going well in the new flat with Philippa and Hope. Living with two girls was eye-opening in lots of ways. For example, I had no idea how absolutely essential candles were. I'd lived a very sheltered life. But it turns out that there must be at least 10 candles in every single room otherwise the house will be cursed. Also, every time a bottle of wine is finished it must not be thrown away. What a waste that would be. Instead, a candle must be shoved in the top of it to create a makeshift lamp and then left on a bookshelf instead of actual books. I was learning so much. For instance, previously I'd assumed that cushions were there to make sofas more comfortable. How ignorant of me! In fact, cushions are absolutely brilliant decorations in their own right and must be scattered *everywhere* in such a volume that they make the actual furniture totally unusable. That's *style*, you see. Gosh, I felt like Eliza Doolittle: an uncouth street urchin being shown the ways of the world by a pair of chic aristocrats dressed in dungarees.

However, the ruinous London rent was pushing me towards financial destitution. It was getting pretty close to the point where I would have to choose between eating food and buying Groupons. Unless I bought food on Groupon. But I wasn't sure whether 3,000 sherbet Dip Dabs or a box of edible underwear even counted as food. However, today I was on my way to King's

Cross to see a psychic. I was hoping that perhaps she might help me find a way out of my impoverished predicament. At the very least I thought she might give me a cup of tea and a biscuit. I hoped so: I was absolutely starving.

Amber opened the door and welcomed me in. She was a very large woman. Less a psychic medium, more a psychic XL. Surely she would have biscuits? As a coldly rational man I was cynical about the whole exercise. Scientific proof for the efficacy of psychics is notoriously absent. But I'd promised myself that I'd take it seriously for as long as possible. I wanted to give Amber a chance. After all, if I was just going to sneer then what would be the point? Amber began by reading my palm. I was asked to rub my hands vigorously together and then present them palm up on the table. Amber told me that I have a rare 'guru loop' underneath my middle finger which suggests I lead people with my sparkling charisma. She said other lines suggested that I've also got a great wit, a kind heart and a massive knob. This was spooky. I was quickly changing my mind about the whole thing.

Next up was clairvoyance. A clairvoyant reads your 'energy' and gets messages from the spirit world. Which basically means dead people were whispering in Amber's ear like flirty ghosts. She was vague about who the spirits were though, which seemed fairly crucial. Like, was it my dead grandad she was talking to or was it Keith Harris and Orville? Anyway, according to Amber, the spirits were suggesting I needed to get some more sleep and look after myself better. But on that particular day I had a cold and I looked terrible. Anyone could have told me to get some more sleep. It soon dawned on me that Amber might just be cold reading. If psychics throw a lot of shit at the wall then some of it is bound to stick. She was saying ambiguous things that were true for most people, so that I would join the dots in my own head and draw profound personal significance. It's classic confirmation bias. We look for information to match the conclusion we want to believe.

Amber then broke down into a coughing fit. 'It was interesting that I started choking up there, Max,' she said. 'That's often because a client swallows situations that they're not totally happy with. It means they're not willing to speak up and tell their truth.' I was getting irritated now. I felt like screaming, 'Yes Amber, you coughing could mean that I'm an emotional doormat who withholds his true feelings to make other people happy. OR IT COULD JUST BE THAT YOU HAVE A COUGH!' But I didn't say anything. I just wanted her to like me, I suppose. But I'd lost confidence in Amber at this stage and was on the verge of walking out. She then announced that it was now time for my tarot card reading so I resolved to stay. After all, there wasn't long left. And then, for the next 10 minutes, my mind was blown. Amber drew out this card:

THE FOOL.

This is The Fool card. The Fool card stands for brave new beginnings. It's the card of infinite possibilities. The bag on the staff is full of the explorer's worldly possessions that he packs up before setting off on a journey he knows not where. As Amber was telling me this all I could think was 'That's me! I'm The Fool!' Mine and Amber's unlikely collision suddenly felt like fate. Maybe I was meant to get this message? Suddenly I felt totally certain that I was doing the right thing. Pissing my savings down the drain didn't feel like a waste, it felt like my duty. It was as if the universe had given me permission. I asked Amber if she had any final advice. She said, 'The Fool tarot card asks you to take a leap of faith and to trust that if you begin a new journey you will find success.' I thanked her heartily, gave her a hug, and then asked if she would make me some toast. She told me it was time to leave.

I bounced out of Amber's flat with certainty in my stride. I couldn't chuck in the Groupon towel now. This was more important than winning a bet with Dave, and it was more important even than winning back Jen's hand. This was about destiny. I'd do whatever it took. I'd max out credit cards. I'd sell a kidney. I'd do anything I needed to keep exploring. Later that afternoon, I returned to the flat to tell the girls what Amber had said. They were both in the living room. Phil reading a copy of *Heat* magazine and Hope on the floor on all fours like a dog, attempting to deal with her trapped wind. I began to wax lyrical about The Fool but they weren't interested in my superstitions of fate and calling. They mainly wanted to know whether it was me who had eaten Hope's Parma ham from the fridge. I confessed immediately, explaining that I'd been famished the night before and promised to replace the ham when I got paid at the end of the week, with meat of equivalent or greater value. In the process I was forced to admit that I'd spent all my food money for the week on a celebrity voicemail from David Hasselhoff. The atmosphere was tense. Then Hope broke wind, which made us all laugh and things were fine after that.

I was a lucky guy. My new flatmates were really supportive of my Groupon lifestyle. That evening they said to me: 'Look, we think it's really great what you're doing, Max, and we're here to get behind you. We want to support you in any way we can. So we've clubbed together and bought you colonic irrigation.'

I smiled politely. Colonic irrigation? This sounded absolutely horrific! But I had no choice. I was legally bound by a subsection of the bet rules to accept any Groupon bought for me. I began to panic. Then I was struck by a calming thought. Perhaps this is the leap of faith that The Fool had demanded? Perhaps this could be a statement of my cast-iron will? After all, it was miles outside of my comfort zone. So I thanked my housemates for their generous gift and off I went, the very next afternoon.

It was comfortably the worst day of my life. I'll be surprised if I'm ever more embarrassed than I was that day at Acqua di Acqua in High Barnet. I went alone. Because believe it or not, it's actually quite hard to find a buddy to do colonic irrigation with you. I mean it's not an easy sell, is it? 'Hi mate, what you up to this afternoon? Fancy having your anus flushed out?' It was so easy to book an appointment, just a few clicks of a mouse, that I hadn't really considered the consequences. I was going to have gallon after gallon of water pumped into my colon, using a tube inserted into my rectum. In doing so 26 years of bum gunk would be disturbed and then flow out of my arse, down a transparent tube which would RUN PAST MY HEAD, like some sort of faecal *Generation Game*.

I had thought of hiding some stuff up there, you know, to surprise the therapist. Something like a small plastic dolphin, or a message in a bottle, or maybe my house keys? Then when they flowed down the tube I could go, 'So that's where they were! What am I like?' But I didn't. The only preparation I did was some light sobbing. On the morning of the colonic I was totally dreading it. I'm ashamed of my bumhole. It's hairy, dark and prone to sweating. Like a badger in an airing cupboard. And for some reason I have this weird suspicion that mine might be worse than everybody else's. In short I wasn't skipping down the street at the prospect of having a total stranger faffing about with it. But I knew this was a test that I had to pass. So off I went.

The clinic was on the first floor of an LA Fitness gym. It was further from the station than I'd imagined and I got lost. I had to ask a local lady for directions, she immediately said 'Oh, you're not having a colonic, are you? They do them there you know! OH MY GOD! Are you having a colonic?' I was like, 'Oh God no! A colonic! How embarrassing! No, no, no, no, I'm here for Zumba.' I arrived just in time. That's when the indignity started. In the reception area, I was handed a form to fill in by the receptionist. At the top was the usual name, address, phone number spiel. And then there were some more personal questions, including: 'How would you describe your stools?' How are you meant to answer that question? 'How would I describe my stools? Through the medium of dance of course!' If my shits went internet dating they would describe themselves as 'Shy but outgoing after a few drinks'. But there wasn't a box for that; it's almost as if they hadn't considered poos going dating. The only options on the form were:

Fat sausage
Skinny sausage
Rabbit droppings
Pebbles
Loose diarrhoea

A lady sat opposite me in the waiting area caught me dithering on the question. She leant over, put her hand on my knee, and proud as Punch loudly announced, 'I put fat sausage!' As if that would help. As if I'd go, 'Oh did you? Fat sausage, you say? Congratulations! Way to go, sister! We should do brunch.' My therapist came over to me and shook my hand: it was my turn. Her name was Katerina, a beautiful young Polish girl with long blonde hair. I really fancied her. She showed me to a small room off the reception area and shut the door. She then explained the science. 'In your colon Mr Dickins, you have 20 foot of intestines, and in your intestines you carry around eight kilograms of poop', before emphasising, 'Which is equivalent to a large cat.' I stared back at her, dumbstruck, before saying: 'I am so glad you put that in cat terms. Because I was lost! Just

to put my mind completely at ease, what's that in hamsters?'

The bed itself was plastic and shaped like a *pedalo*. Around halfway up was a stiff plastic tube. Katerina handed me a sachet of lubricant. 'What you need to do is lube up the tube with this, and insert it into your anus. When you're done, ring the bell.' This is going to sound mad but I was delighted at this news. I thought she was going to

have to stick the pipe in for me, but now I was saved from this particular embarrassment. She left and I got undressed from the waist down. Now with the tube up my arse and a white towel concealing my offal, I called her back in.

I had never felt more exposed. Here I was with a tube up my bum, legs akimbo, with a Polish woman about to fill my intestines full of liquid. She had her hand on the tap. 'Ready?' she said. I nodded and she turned the tap on. Water was now flooding my colon. 'When you feel cramps in your stomach I want you to push,' she said, looking me straight in the eyes. 'Like when you go to the toilet.' About a minute passed. I couldn't feel a thing. 'Are you sure the tube's in?' I said. She nodded and said 'Oh yes, it's *very* deep,' in a tone of voice that suggested I'd done that on purpose. Katerina turned up the pressure. Another minute passed; I still couldn't feel anything. I tried to make small talk, 'So do you live round here?' I said. She ignored me and turned the tap up yet again. She seemed genuinely worried at this stage, baffled by how much water I could take in my arse without feeling any pain.

Suddenly I could feel the cramps, like I'd done too many sit-ups. 'I can feel it!' I said, absolutely delighted. 'Push! Push!' she screamed. And I really tried, but nothing was coming out. I really felt like I was letting her down. I actually felt embarrassed that I couldn't shit myself in front of this gorgeous woman. 'Sorry,' I said. 'I'm normally really good at this.' About five seconds later I exploded. Katerina, now stood at the end of the bed, started cheering. 'Yeah! Well done! Big chunk!' She high fived me. I started crying tears of joy. I had finally got the hang of it: you wait to be filled up to the extent that you cramp and then you contract your diaphragm, pushing the water out of your arse – essentially turning your digestive system into a set of bellows.

So what does it feel like? Well, I've never been bummed, but a colonic is like being bummed by the sea. Sometimes so much water goes in that you feel like vomiting, as if you are about to turn into one of those cherub fountains where water goes in your bum and straight out your mouth. Katerina was obviously impressed. 'What have you seen? Toxins? Lumps? Gas?' 'Bit of everything,' I giggled, barely containing my excitement. I was showing off now. The thought genuinely crossed my mind: maybe I could ask her out? Then I did a massive fart and thought better of it. Katerina could see I was having fun, so she left me to it, leaving the room. But not before opening the window slightly ajar to help with the smell, which as you can imagine was fairly haunting. However, the window made the room very draughty and suddenly the door blew open, meaning that everyone in reception could now see directly up my arse. I had 12 pairs of shocked eyes trained on me. I began ringing the bell like mad, screaming Katerina's name. She was nowhere to be seen. I thought, 'This can't get any worse.' But at the end of the reception area I saw the handle on the front door beginning to twist. And yet another person walked in. It was the woman who had given me directions earlier. AT THIS STAGE I WOULD HAVE HAPPILY SHOT MYSELF. She stared at me, I stared at her, totally lost for words. She eventually said, 'Oh … was Zumba full?' And at last Katerina comes to my rescue, slamming the door shut. I began to cry again, this time in despair.

Walking home, my bowels felt light and relaxed. It felt like I'd had a big poo, but to the power of ten. The first meal I had post-irrigation was a red Thai curry, which was a major strategic error. The chilli stung my colon like aftershave on a freshly razored face. My digestive tract offered little resistance. It was like dropping a marble down a lift shaft. Colonic irrigation was clearly absolutely horrendous. But weirdly it didn't put me off My Groupon Adventure. In fact it empowered me, because it had been such a humiliating experience that I realised virtually nothing in life could be more embarrassing. I was suddenly immune to making an idiot of myself and consequently I felt fearless. This was what I was finding with my Groupon experiences. Every time I tried something new – something that on the surface level seemed only shallow and fun – I got a secondary psychological benefit too. I had come to realise that My Groupon Adventure was a daft project with profound positive externalities. Spending an hour of my life soiling myself in front of a stranger had made me a better person. And I never thought I'd say that.

Chapter Nine

By the early summer of 2014 I had exhausted Groupon's vast vault of offers. So voracious had my consumption been, so ravenous my appetite for adventure that there was literally nothing left. I had defeated the boss. I had completed Groupon. Yes, there was the odd offer aimed at only women or children that I'd yet to do, but it wasn't for lack of trying. For example, I sent 15 separate emails to a pole dancing class only to be rejected on every occasion. This was despite my very generous offer to attend with a mangina. So there was only one thing for it: I had to break America. The most rudimentary of research had shown me that Groupon was huge across the pond. It was an unconquered cornucopia of discounts. Now I convinced myself that it was my humble duty as torch carrier for the spontaneous to invade. It was time to stick it to Uncle Sam. The Fool was about to go on tour.

I settled on the idea of a road-trip. I had fantasies of Kerouac; a wandering nomad with a poet's heart. But I needed a partner. Who was to be my Dean Moriarty? So naturally I asked Dave. 'Who the fuck is Dean Moriarty?' he said, before eating one of the 10 Monster Munch he'd placed like a ring on each of his fingers. 'He's the hero from *On the Road*,' I explained, 'An icon of the Beat Generation.' Dave's face was blank. I'd just named someone who was in neither Steps nor

Destiny's Child and he was confused. I can always tell when Dave is confused because he has a special expression on his face. Like there's a fly stuck behind his forehead and he's trying to look at it. 'It doesn't matter,' I said. 'I need a travelling buddy. I wondered if you might like to join me?' Dave was still unmoved. 'Come on mate, let's face it, tramps like us, baby we were born to run.' Bruce Springsteen lyrics were my DEFCON 1 tactic; and I'd smashed the glass and gone nuclear far earlier than planned. But it worked. Like an egg cracked into a hot frying pan, a bright smile suddenly coalesced over Dave's face as he imagined what we might get up to. 'Alright,' he said, 'I'll do it. Two rules though: no camping and no gay stuff.' 'Deal,' I said. 'Deal,' he said, before chomping on some of his pickled onion flavour bling.

We set about planning our route. We were to fly into New Orleans and then depart from Denver, Colorado seven days later. It would be a huge amount of driving but we had a lot to pack in. There was an excellent reason to end in Colorado, but I hadn't told Dave the good news yet. Colorado was home to the world's only alligator wrestling class and I had booked us two tickets. This was to be my most ludicrous and extreme challenge yet. Get through this and I could definitely herald myself as a new man. Colonic irrigation had been a terrifying prospect but this had raised the stakes. This was a symbolic moment. It was a chance to look my demon square in the eye and destroy it forever. But we had a lot more Groupons to cram in first.

We spent our first night sampling the jazz clubs of New Orleans. The experimental nature of the players' improvisations was the musical manifestation of the philosophy I'd been seeking to embrace. Some worked, some didn't, but it was exhilarating to watch them jump off a cliff. The next day we set off for Austin in Texas. 'I've made us a playlist for the trip,' said Dave, plugging his iPod into the stereo system. 'Today is the start of your musical education. Part One, Module A – girl bands of the 90s.' Consequently the 12-hour drive into Texas felt like 12 days. Were you aware that Eternal released four whole albums? I wish I wasn't either. We drove west on the freeway, eventually leaving the fruity wetlands of Louisiana behind and crossing the border into Texas.

Texas is the behemoth state. If it were an independent country it would rank as the 40th biggest in the world. Much of it is a dusty void. Tyre shards littered the hard shoulder. Gigantic roadkill festered in the heat. The arid desert landscape was bare but for the occasional rusty goods train, which would snake diligently past us on the parallel track. Every five miles we'd see an enormous anti-abortion billboard and turn-offs to luminescent fast food hamlets. The earth appeared totally flat. The beige freeway a vapour trail bisecting an empty horizon. Every other radio station was playing country music now. Eventually we began to see oil wells, the black nodding donkeys humbly going about their extraction. Finally we were closing in on civilisation.

We arrived into Austin close to midnight. If you're wondering what Austin is like, they sell beer in the pharmacy. That's all you need to know. We were here for guns. Texans take the second amendment very seriously. Guns outnumber people three to one in the Lone Star State. So I thought: when in Rome, and bought a Groupon which allowed us to take the four hours of training necessary to qualify for a concealed weapons licence. Just four hours basic tuition was all you needed to be able to walk around town with a gun in your pocket. The venue was Red's Indoor Gun Range, which was opposite the Texan Department of Public Safety. Who says Americans don't do irony?

I went up to the counter and presented our vouchers. 'Are you a citizen of the United States of America?' asked the moustached man sternly. 'No, we're from England,' I said. 'I'm actually Welsh,' added Dave unhelpfully. 'I'm afraid only US citizens may hold a concealed weapon licence. Sorry,' said the man. 'Hey!' said Dave, 'The only concealed weapon I've got is MY PENIS!' Dave offered up a high five but both of us left him hanging. Dave, though, was unfazed: 'Hey, is that a gun in your pocket or are you just pleased to see me?' 'That is a 12mm semi-automatic handgun,' replied the man matter-of-factly. 'Would it be OK if we just used the gun range?' I said. 'Absolutely. Right this way, sir.'

Two minutes later I had the cold black metal of a Glock 9mm pistol in my hand. In the other I had a box of bullets. I was also wearing transparent goggles, so I looked like a chemistry teacher with an unorthodox way of maintaining discipline in the classroom. The range made me anxious. It was the noise mainly. A hellish din of gunfire. But it was also the precariousness of my safety. At the moment everyone else was pointing their guns at the paper effigies in front of them, but all it would take would be one madman to turn 90 degrees to his left and he could slay all of us in seconds. I was also fretful about my own incompetence. The demonstration of the gun had lasted no longer than two minutes. It included the pithy advice, 'Don't shoot yourself.' I made sure I wrote that bit down. The last thing I wanted to do was to forget to not shoot myself. But what if I slipped and actually did end up killing myself? Or someone else? The responsibility was gnawing.

I had a tiny gun in the grand scheme of things – the man in the booth next to me had a rifle big enough to bring down an Airbus – but I was immediately struck by the power of it. The recoil knocked me back each time I pulled the trigger. It took me half an hour to unload 10 rounds into the 2D terrorist pinned up 12 feet in front of me. If he had been real, he would have been shaken but I think he would have lived. When I returned to the shop I found Dave chatting to our friend from earlier. His name was Kevin. 'A Japanese general once said that he would never invade America because behind every blade of grass was an American with a gun,' said Kevin. Which sounded like a rubbish hiding place to me, but this is the nub of the American obsession with guns. It is the paranoid fear of attack. 'How many guns have you got?' I asked. 'What do you mean? On me now? In my car? At home?' I hadn't thought of the categories. 'I've got loads of guns. Guns for fun. Guns for sport. Guns for protection. Guns for when I'm running errands.' This was a niche I did not realise existed. Guns for errands. Is this how some guns are advertised? 'Popping out for bog roll? Try the new Glock fun-sized pistol.' 'The only time I don't carry a gun,' continued Kevin, 'is when I go out drinking. I don't want to end up doing anything I'll regret.' 'What do you carry then?' I asked. 'A hunting knife,' he said. That's OK then.

Our next stop was a tiny redneck town called Cleburne, a mere four hours down the road. We were here for our next Groupon. I'd bought us tickets to the Johnson County Sheriff's Posse PRCA Pro-Rodeo. The grass car park was slammed with pickup trucks shimmering in the late evening sun. Our hatchback cringed as I manoeuvred him between two of these ogres. People stared. Everybody at the rodeo had donned cowboy hats, jeans, boots and a plaid shirt. I was wearing flip-flops and shorts; Dave was wearing a T-shirt with an alien on the front with the caption 'Take Me to Your Dealer' written on it. We stood out and they hadn't even heard our accents yet. 'Two tickets to the rodeo, please,' I said with as much obsequious British charm as I could muster. The sour-faced teenager chewing gum at the box office stared back at me like a horse watching Chekhov. 'Waaat d'yew saaaayyy?' she drawled. 'Ummm ... well ... I'd like to buy two tickets for the rodeo please,' I said a bit slower. She suddenly became very nervous, hands shaking, face reddening, eyes swelling into awe-struck moons. I think she thought I was a Prince. She gave me the tickets. 'Twenty dollars,' she said breathlessly. I gave her the money and we shuffled into the arena behind a man so fat that he was dragging along an oxygen tank behind him as he moved. Welcome to America.

I say 'arena'. It could only have held a couple of thousand people. The white stands framing a field of churned dirt. Country tunes pummelled out from columns of speakers. The rodeo announcer broadcasted bombastically. He was called West Huggins. Every man in America seems to have a name like this: epic sounding and onomatopoeic. But it's a strange choice as a parent to name your child 'West'. Unless there's a relevance that I've missed. Perhaps he's one half of conjoined twins and he and East Huggins had since been separated. The rodeo seemed a family affair with the stands packed with the cowboys' wives and sisters, who were often the same person.

West Huggins continued to get us pumped up and then announced that if we bought a $10 raffle ticket we could 'win a cat'. This really was a bizarre place. 'Let's get a raffle ticket!' beamed Dave. 'I don't want to win a cat, Dave. Where are we going to put it? We can't just keep it in the car.' 'Why not?' he said. 'It will cook.' 'We could leave the air-conditioning on?' 'No. Anyway, even if it did manage to survive the trip, how would we get it back to the UK?' 'On a plane stupid! Jesus,' said Dave as if I'd just dropped a massive clanger. 'You can't just put a cat in your luggage, Dave.' 'I'll put it in my carry-on. They'll look at it and think it's a pencil case or something. Or it can sit on my lap. I'll give it a disguise and tell the air stewards that it's a baby.' The heat was getting to Dave and so I packed him off to buy us a Pepsi.

Ten minutes later, Dave returned with two cans of soda and 15 raffle tickets. West Huggins was now banging on about freedom and how America was the greatest nation on earth. He asked any serving or ex-service men and women to stand up. A man sat next to us rose to his feet. He was in civvies but had a handgun in a holster attached to his belt. 'Shake them by the hand and say thank you,' said West. The crowd erupted into applause. 'Only two people have died for our freedom,' said West, 'the brave servicemen of the United States of America and Jesus Christ.' We all gave Jesus Christ a round of applause too because he's a good lad. West then cued up the Hovis theme tune and asked us to recite a prayer with him. 'God bless America,' he said. Finally we all rose to our feet once more and sang the 'Star Spangled Banner'. 'Don't forget to try our world famous Rodeo Burger,' added West. The past five minutes had summed up Texas in a nutshell.

Finally it was show time. There was bareback bronco riding, team roping, and steer wrestling. This was a ludicrous event where a cowboy on horseback chases a young bull before jumping from his horse onto its back and then wrestles it to the ground. Absolutely bonkers. The second half of the rodeo was all about bull riding, which is statistically the most dangerous sport in the world with an injury rate double that of its nearest competitor, American football. Riders are put on enormous bulls bred for bucking and win a point if they can stay on it for a mere eight seconds. Most fail and are flung off violently into even greater danger. Because they are now at the mercy of the bull. A 'rodeo clown' in face paint and red waistcoat jumps in the way to distract the animal for long enough for the stricken rider to make his getaway. It doesn't always work out like that though. We saw a rabid bull toss a cowboy around like a dirty sock. I'll be honest, that was the best bit.

This was all after the half-time show, though. 'Would all the ladies over eighteen years old please come out onto the arena,' boomed West Huggins. Twenty Daisy Dukes strutted onto the soil. 'Give me a cheer if you'd like to win 50 bucks!' he hollered, drawing cheers of delight from the girls. 'OK! Release the bull!' said West. 'You've got to be fucking joking!' I said to Dave, as a full-sized bull raced into the arena splitting the sea of girls. It was enormous. Like a Hummer made of beef. There was a ribbon tied to one of its horns. 'Grab the ribbon and win the cash!' chortled West. In any other place on earth the girls would have said, 'Screw this. You're having a laugh if you think I'm running after a bull to win 50 dollars'. But this is Texas. En masse the harem gave chase. Twenty seconds later I saw an eighteen-year-old girl smashed by a bull and thrown 10 feet into the air. This was met not with screams of terror by the crowd, but by yells of ecstasy. The girl flumped onto the baked clods and lay motionless for a few seconds. I covered my mouth with my hand. She looked dead. Suddenly though, she leapt back to her feet, both fists in the air, delighted at what had just happened. The crowd went wild. But before she had time to drop her hands back down by her sides, she was gored again by the bull. I was beginning to think that maybe I'd taken the easy option with alligator wrestling.

It was raffle time. On the gantry West Huggins stuck his hand into the tombola. Dave spread his tickets out like a Chinese fan. 'OK the winning ticket is number 105. Number 105. Would the winner please make themselves known to the box office so you can claim your prize.' 'I don't believe it,' said Dave, 'I've won a fucking cat'. 'You've got to be kidding,' I said, grabbing at his tickets. 'Look. There it is. We've won a cat.' I went to wait in the car while Dave collected his winnings. I needed some time to calm down a bit. Ten minutes later Dave joined me, empty-handed and looking sad. 'I didn't win a cat,' he said. 'Ah well, it's for the best,' I said, mightily relieved. 'Was there a mistake with your ticket?' 'No,' he said, 'I won the raffle. It's just I didn't win a cat.' I stared at him for a bit. 'What are you on about, Dave?' He pointed up at his head. He was wearing an 'I love Texas' cap. We'd misheard West's southern accent. 'He didn't say cat, he said ...' I started to laugh. 'It's not actually that funny,' said Dave, 'I really wanted a cat.' 'How many tickets did you buy again?' I said. '15. I bought 15.' 'So you've basically spent $150 on a cap?' 'Just drive, will you,' he said.

We stayed overnight in Cleburne before another long drive to Roswell in New Mexico the next day. Roswell is famous for being the site of an alleged UFO crash in July 1947. We visited the museum the following morning, but that evening we dined on Cheesy Puffs in our grimy motel room. We had no choice. Everywhere in Roswell shuts at 8pm. I turned on the TV whilst Dave used my laptop to look for new Groupon deals. Groupon is different in America. They sell a much wider, weirder array of stuff. 'Would you be up for getting your Las Vegas stripper licence?' asked Dave. 'I'd be up for it but we're not going anywhere near Vegas, mate,' I said, mightily relieved. 'That's a shame,' he said. 'Yeah. I'm gutted mate.' 'OK ... how about a "Fetish Fantasy Inflatable Wrestling Ring"? It comes with a free gallon of lubricant?' 'I thought you said no gay stuff, Dave?' 'Oh, hang on. It takes ten days to deliver. We'll be gone by then.' Because that was the only thing wrong with that deal.

'They've got 75% off circumcision if you fancy it?' said Dave. 'No thanks,' I said skipping channels. Dave started laughing. 'What's funny?' I said. 'Well,' said Dave, reaching for his wallet, 'if I buy you the offer you have to do it, otherwise you fail and incur

Groupon Deal from Hell!' Shit. Shit. Shit. 'Mate. Please don't ...' Dave was already dialling in his debit card details. 'Dave, please don't,' I said. 'Look, you've been saying you want to lose a bit of weight. This is the perfect opportunity.' Dave ceremoniously pressed enter on the keyboard. 'Done.' He said, before breaking out in hysterics. I suddenly needed a wee. I was soon to lose my foreskin and maybe unconsciously I wanted to spend as much time with it as possible. 'Oh no!' I heard Dave's frustrated shouts through the bathroom wall. I finished washing my hands and walked back into the twin room. 'What it is?' 'They've rejected my card!' Suddenly his phone vibrated. Dave read the text message out loud, 'We suspect fraudulent transactions on your debit card. Please ring our fraud department as soon as possible.' Now I was in hysterics. 'No wonder your bank think it's fraudulent Dave! You've just bought a circumcision in New Mexico, and you normally spend all your money on 90s reunion gigs in London.'

Relieved, I laid back down on my bed and returned my attention to the television. A sewage of ludicrous medical advertisements rushed at me through the screen. Adverts selling medical products that solved invented problems. '*8 out of 10 men have dry eyeballs. You're a winner in every other part of your life, so why not with your eyeballs? Try new Sprozium eye-lubricating spray. In controlled trials, 70% of patients reported experiencing wetter eyes as a result of using Sprozium. Side effects may include – but may not be limited to – nausea, headaches, backache, coughing, a craving for yoghurt, swelling of the ankles, a Japanese accent, heart palpitations, suddenly enjoying East European gypsy music, vomiting, thinking you are Bruce Forsyth, suicide, inability to get through a conversation without making a pun, and diarrhoea.*'

If it wasn't a medical advert, it was a commercial for a car lot.

Americans love adverts that feature the owner of the business bombastically screaming at you down the barrel of the camera whilst wearing a baseball cap with their name on it. *'Hi, I'm Big Jack from Big Jack's car superstore! This weekend we've got 80% off all cars! I'm crazy! What am I doing? 80% off cars? Seriously: somebody shoot me!'* I channel hopped once more, thinking it was perhaps unwise for Big Jack to tempt fate. Dave piped up again: 'How about this: "Male Stripogram: make your bachelorette party go with a bang with your own personal show!"' And I felt genuinely sad. Imagine selling yourself on Groupon like a piece of meat. It was so undignified. But this was America, the country where everything is for sale. As long as you've got money, you can get whatever you want, wherever you want, whenever you want. Unless you're staying in Roswell and it's after 8pm, obviously. 'I'm not buying myself a male stripper, Dave,' I said. 'Sorry.'

The next day was alligator day. We'd only been in America for a week but by this stage I'd begun talking in an embarrassing mid-Atlantic accent and unconsciously using American words like 'dude' and 'douchebag' and 'extra-large'. Being on the road for so long had started to take its toll on my diet too. A barrage of Burger King, McDonald's and Denny's had bunged me up. I would need another colonic when I got home. But the colonic could prove to be superfluous. I would be wrestling alligators in around four hours and so there was a fair chance I would shit myself anyway. That morning I coyly dialled the destination into the sat nav. 'Where are we going?' asked Dave, increasingly irascible about being kept in the dark. 'The Rocky Mountains,' I said. But Dave had already stopped listening and was now fiddling with his iPod. We were onto Part 5, Module E: Mel B's solo work. Luckily, five minutes later Dave had fallen asleep in the passenger seat, mouth gaping like a gormless sex doll. I turned on the radio instead. It was preset to a station called Bible Views

Radio. A preacher calling himself Dr Ron Baskey was claiming that Al Gore had invented the internet, that earthquakes were caused by vegetarians, and that 'God created Adam and Eve. He didn't create Adam and Steve'. Meanwhile, I drove past a lorry branded 'S.T.I. Deliveries'. It was good to be abroad.

Having reached Colorado Alligators I parked the car and shook Dave awake. He had a crescent of drool on his T-shirt. 'We're here,' I said. 'What do you mean "here"?' he said. 'What does "here" mean?' 'We're at an alligator park. We're about to wrestle the alligators.' I said. Dave slapped me in the face. I cowered and cupped my stinging cheek. 'Sorry, it was a reflex,' he said. Dave was terrified. I tried to put him at ease. 'Look, if it was really dangerous they wouldn't let us do it.' We walked into the reception area. Stood there were two local lads who had just taken the class. They were covered in blood. 'How was it, guys?' I asked. 'Yeah, man. It's pretty intense. Apparently last week someone had their hand bitten off.' Dave looked like he was about to faint. 'Hey … are you guys from England?' the other one asked. 'We're from London,' I explained. 'Cool. Do you guys know Harry Potter?' he said. 'Oh yeah. He was my fag at Eton,' I said sarcastically. They both nodded in a way that said, 'Yes, that makes sense actually'.

The lady at the desk presented us with release forms. These waived Colorado Alligator from any legal responsibility in the event of our injury or death. Dave and I reluctantly signed on the dotted line. So now, beyond basic moral concern, they had absolutely no stake in whether we lived or died. This *laissez faire* attitude to liability was the reason we were here. Colorado is the only place in the entire world where you can wrestle alligators because of a unique law that puts the burden of risk in agricultural pursuits on the customer and not the provider. Our health insurance was null and void. We were on our own.

Dave and I walked around the farm. It was a system of interlocking man-made swamps filled with alligators, some of which were submerged beneath the murky green with only their sinister black eyes protruding above the surface. Others lounged on the banks sunbathing in their corrugated body armour, like long artichokes, with smug grins that said 'There is almost nothing in the world that we could not kill'. Many were as long as 16 feet. There was one alligator called Morris who had come here to retire after spending 25 years working in the movie business. He'd appeared in *Happy Gilmour*, *Dr Doolittle* and many more. I'd be lying if I said that it wasn't depressing to find a reptile with a better showreel than me.

Back at base camp, a short fat man with a toby jug face and goatee barrelled in. He was shaped like a tea urn and dressed in shorts and T-shirt. 'Hey guys, I'm Drew. I'll be your instructor today!' he said with typical American enthusiasm. 'Are you a professional alligator wrestler?' asked Dave. 'No way! I'm just a volunteer! I've taken the class a couple times and now they let me teach it for some reason!' he said. 'I run a dog's home normally. But an alligator's bite is two hundred times more powerful than a pit bull's'. Dave's sphincter audibly loosened. 'Nice cap, by the way,' he added.

We ventured out to the first swamp. It was time to dance with death. Drew said that there are only two rules when it comes to alligator wrestling: don't hesitate and don't let go. You've got to grab it and hold on for dear life. Otherwise it will escape and come back for revenge. The technique sounds deceptively simple. You wade in and approach the alligator from behind, grabbing its thick, leathery tail with both hands before dragging it out of the swamp and onto the shore. There you jump on its back and get both hands on top of the neck, sitting on its spine, with your feet up in front of the front legs. Next you work your hands down beneath its jaw and pull the head up so it's pointing at the sky vertically. In this position there's nothing they can do. The physics are in your favour. Of course the alligators don't just submissively let you get away with all this. They don't see it as kinky foreplay, some irreverent reptilian BDSM. No, they fight back, slapping their tail from side to side, desperately trying to flip around and bite you. What's not to like?

This was the moment of truth. Our lives are defined by how we react to certain events and despite bringing it all on myself I knew this was one of them. In front of me was a door. Between me and the door were lots of hungry alligators, and on the other side of the door was personal transformation. I just had to take a deep breath and walk through. 'The alligators in this first swamp are only eight and a half feet long,' said Drew. The world's tallest man comes in at eight foot three. Drew waded in and demonstrated as Dave and I watched through our fingers. Having successfully tamed it on the bank, Drew leapt up off the gator and let it slip off back into the water. 'Right, who wants to go first?' he asked. Dave pointed at me. 'Yep … errr … I'd love to, Drew,' I said. 'Cool. In you go then,' he said. 'What about this one?' I said, pointing at an alligator four feet away from me on the shoreline. 'Why don't I just jump on that one?' 'That's Steve,' said Drew. 'He's blind and only has three legs.' 'Perfect. I'll take that one,' I said, absolutely delighted. Drew put his hand on my shoulder. 'No. Get in the swamp. Stop being such a pussy.' A braying crowd had now gathered. It had turned into *The Hunger Games* meets *The Really Wild Show*.

In I went. 'If you feel an alligator next to you in the swamp, stand like a tree and play dead,' said Drew flippantly. I approached an alligator that was submerged in front of me. I tentatively grabbed at its tail and it escaped, slapping my arms violently with his leathery appendage, knocking me off my feet and into the swamp. Submerged deep in the water, I began to panic. My ears, nose and mouth filled with liquid. All I could think was 'I'VE FALLEN IN! I'VE FUCKING FALLEN INTO AN ALLIGATOR-INFESTED SWAMP!' I could hear the muffled sound of the crowd screaming. I stared out into the warm, cloudy, translucent green. This brief moment in time elongated by fear. I managed to struggle to my feet, choking on the tepid, fetid water. 'Don't hesitate and don't let go!' lambasted Drew. Gasping for air, I nodded and waded forwards, snorting algae out of my nose. I hadn't travelled halfway across the world to give up now.

The crowd shouted encouragement. If they didn't get to see me eaten by an alligator then watching me successfully wrestling one was clearly their second best option. As I pressed deeper into the swamp I could feel my bare feet sinking deeper and deeper into the mud, the disturbed silt floating like tadpoles around my shins. This time I got one. It was going tonto, spasming violently and horizontally as I reversed backwards to the dry bank. I hauled the lethal luggage onto the shore, using every bit of my meagre body strength. Drew was screaming, 'Jump on her! Jump on her!' This was a very counter-intuitive thought – to voluntarily throw myself onto the back of an alligator. But the alternative was worse, to have this furious brute turn back and eat me for lunch. I dived on top to huge cheers. The gator growled but I had her where I wanted her now. Chalk up one for man versus nature.

'Don't put your fingers near her jaw!' warned Drew as he inspected the studded body for wounds. This was part of the drill. Being dangerous psychopaths, alligators spend a lot of their time attacking one another and so they need treatment lest they die of an infection in the swamp. And so it comes down to heroes like me to drag them out of the depths so they might be healthy enough to one day kill someone else. 'Yep, she's fine,' said Drew. 'Jump up and let her go.' I stood up off her and backed away carefully as she slithered back into the brine. I had cuts all over my legs and blood streaming from my right knee. The sheer danger of what I had got myself into had dawned on me for the first time. Drew seemed unhinged. The gator park was to health and safety what Donald Trump is to toupees. It felt like an accident waiting to happen. I thought of the man who lived with grizzly bears in Alaska. For years he lived close to the bears and against the odds they all got on. People said, 'See! It is possible for man and beast to coexist happily!' And then inevitably one day he got eaten by a bear. I thought too of the guy who invented the Segway and then died when he accidentally drove it off a cliff. My point is: if you play with fire then one day you're going to get burnt. I prayed that today wouldn't be that day.

Drew's heavily pregnant Mexican girlfriend Rosana had arrived swamp side to watch with their young son. Now it was Dave's turn and he reticently paddled around the edges of the swamp like a shy teenager avoiding talking to a girl at a disco. 'Come on sweetheart! What's up? You a man or a mouse?' goaded Drew to the obvious amusement of his wife (and me). Dave forced a laugh from his quivering lips and then pressed on a bit deeper. He made a half-hearted grab at a stray tail but the alligator swam off easily. Drew rolled his eyes. 'Rosana, show him.' Rosana nodded casually and then vaulted over the fence into the swamp, stomach swollen with child, and powered into the water. Within seconds she had an alligator in her tiny hands and was pulling it ashore. 'That's my girl!' said Drew, as Rosana and her unborn baby dropped down heartily onto its back. These people were insane. What sort of husband lets his heavily pregnant wife tussle with an alligator? What sort of pregnant woman acquiesces? Extraordinary. It makes you wonder: what do these two do on Valentine's Day? Play *Twister* with a wolf?

For the next two hours Drew led us from swamp to swamp

and we wrestled bigger and bigger alligators. Dave had got the hang of it now and we had a growing confidence that was beginning to look like complacency. That was to change very quickly. The final challenge involved us walking through a chest deep swamp to a raised bank on the opposite side. 'There are 65 alligators in this swamp so be careful,' said Drew. Dave and I looked at each other with bewilderment. 'This must be a wind-up?' I said to Dave. 'The man is mentally ill,' he said. We looked up and Drew was halfway across the swamp with a length of blue rope in his hand, which he was fashioning into a lasso. 'I'm not sure I can do this,' said Dave. 'Come one,' I said, 'this is the last one.' We joined Drew on the bank and he told us to follow him into the depths of the swamp one final time. We would find a 12-foot alligator he said, lasso its jaw, drag it ashore and then wrestle it. Now if at this point someone had asked me for a list of things I'd rather do, then French kissing a baboon, nipple clamping a sumo wrestler, or going up behind Mike Tyson at an ATM and sticking my thumb up his bum, would all be on it. Those were all less terrifying choices. But unfortunately they weren't on the menu and so into the swamp I went.

Alligators aren't mad about having their snouts lassoed. In fact, I'd go as far as saying that they think it's majorly shit. This bad boy wasn't shy in letting us know either, as three of us struggled to pull it ashore. Again, it felt totally bizarre to be physically straining every sinew to drag a massive dangerous animal *towards* me. We were struggling with the task. But Rosana clearly thought: in for a penny, in for a pound, and joined us in this macabre tug of war, tipping the balance in our favour and we managed to heave the monster onto the beach. 'Don't let the rope go slack!' warned Drew as Dave and I let the rope go slack. Suddenly the alligator yanked away and managed to escape the noose, sweeping around behind us, jaw gaping. We all leapt to safety as it snapped down on the bag in Drew's hand before taking it off into the deep. I watched as it death rolled with the bag in its mouth and then took it to the bottom of the swamp to eat it. I looked at Dave. That could have been us.

Driven on by Drew we went back in again and found another monster, this time successfully getting him onto the shore and installing me precariously on its back. He was called Elvis. Drew started tapping it on the snout, provoking it to open its jaw furiously. Drew laughed and then played a little game where he would try to touch the alligator's tongue and remove his hand before its mouth slammed shut. This was the final nail. No further questions, my lord. Drew was certifiably crazy. He then said, 'Do you want to ride him back into the swamp?' 'Sorry, Drew?' I said. 'Do you want to ride this alligator back into the swamp?' he said. 'What? Like a hovercraft? Won't I basically aid and abet my own murder?' I asked. 'But you've come all this way?' he said. 'Yeah, go on mate,' said Dave, who was notably not sat on a 12-foot alligator. Six weeks previously I'd seen an offer for a 'Write Your Own Will Kit' on Groupon and jokingly left everything I owned to Dave. Now he was seeing his chance to claim the bounty.

This was peer pressure. Just like that time when I was 14 on a school history trip to St Albans and I was bullied into smoking a makeshift spliff stuffed with leaves. 'Alright,' I said. 'I'll do it.' I am nothing if not predictably pathetic. That's my biggest weakness in life. I'm just not very assertive. I can never say 'no' to anything. At university I actually ended up with a boyfriend for a bit – just out of politeness. Drew nodded at me. I nodded back and then lifted my weight slightly, allowing Elvis to bolt for the water and cut elegantly into the surf with me clinging on for dear life. Elvis had left the building. I was not just being pulled into the swamp, but across a threshold. I had walked through the door. I had changed. My nerve lasted for roughly 10 seconds and then I let go and breathlessly clambered back onto the bank. Drew high fived me. Dave and I shared a hug. Rosana started doing press-ups with a fag in her mouth. We'd survived.

On the way out, the owner of the park toasted our courage. He offered a handshake, extending out his right arm, which was also his only arm. I hope he never falls into the swamp. He'll only be able to swim in circles. Back in the car Dave promptly fell asleep again. But as I drove away with the sun slipping slowly behind the Rockies, I felt an exhausted, satisfied peace. I'd climbed a steep mountain, planted my flag at the summit, and was stood above the clouds basking in how far I'd come. Flying to America to wrestle alligators was a long way from defrosting and then eating an entire birthday cake by myself. Our final destination was another crummy motel in the suburbs of Denver. Yet despite the scratchy linen, the heavy smell of stale cigarette smoke and the loud air-conditioning unit, I slept perfectly. My mission felt complete. The rest would be a lap of honour. That evening I texted Jen a selfie of me kissing an alligator. I was a man transformed – she would have to admit it. I had finally become spontaneous.

Chapter Ten

Four days later I was back in Blighty and stood on the doorstep of my parents' house. I'd come over to show off my alligator photos. If this didn't make them proud, then nothing would. I rang the bell and Dad answered the door looking agitated. 'Keep your voice down!' he whispered. 'We've got eight Germans upstairs!' I stared back at him aghast. My father has always maintained a bizarre suspicion of Germany and now he'd taken hostages. 'Dad … what's going on? What have you done?' I said, worried. 'What do you mean?' he said, 'Oh! The Krauts! Yes. Sorry. They're B&B guests. Look, you better come in and take a seat before they put their towels down on the sofa.' My father led me through to the kitchen, where my mother was clearing away the breakfast plates. 'They're actually quite nice,' said Mum, genuinely surprised. 'I said to them this morning, I said, "we normally do bacon and eggs for breakfast, but we've got some sausages in especially for you". Which I think they appreciated.' 'Mum, that's so racist!' I said. 'What's racist about that? It's a lovely gesture, that's what it is. They were organic.' 'What else have you done? Replaced the Bibles in the bedside tables with copies of *Mein Kampf*?' I said. 'Don't be so stupid!' she said. 'You can't get your hands on *Mein Kampf* for love nor money these days.' 'Errr, yes you can,' said Dad. who was now sat like Winston Churchill, with a sausage perched in-between his lips as if a cigar. 'You can buy it on Amazon. Terrible reviews.' 'Dad, why the hell were you looking up *Mein Kampf* on Amazon?' I said. 'I got there accidentally. I was looking at Jeremy Clarkson's new book and there was a link. "Customers who bought this item, also bought *Mein Kampf*."

My parents weren't impressed with the alligator wrestling pictures. 'You're a fucking idiot,' said Dad, pointing his sausage at me for emphasis. Mum was more concerned with my love life. My cousin's wedding was just eight weeks away now, and I was still without a 'plus one'. 'How come you can kiss an alligator but you can't get a girlfriend?' she said. Unfortunately my mother had a point. Maybe it was time I took some tentative steps back into the dating game? After all, everyone wants what they can't have, right? I still wanted Jen back, there was no doubt about that. But a few photos of me on Facebook with other girls wouldn't do any harm. I needed her to think I was moving on, that I was slipping away from her. Then she would be forced to realise that the grass actually isn't greener. I'd done the hard bit – I'd become spontaneous. Now I had another plan too: I needed to look *desired*.

It was time to put myself out there. I was single and ready to mingle. So I signed up to an online dating site. But I wanted an edge. I needed to find a way to stand out from the other guys. I needed as a USP. An X factor. So I became a lord. Not many men could compete with that, surely? As a bona fide Lord of the Realm I consequently received the Deeds of Entitlement to the magnificent Dunans Castle in the Scottish Highlands. I was suddenly on the property ladder! And now that I was a lord I was legally entitled to use my new peerage in whatever ways I saw fit. In fact, I rang up Santander and got them to change the name on my bills to Lord Dickins.

Alright, I bought my Lordship on Groupon for 12 quid. But the women on Match.com didn't need to know that did they? I WAS A LORD! And I would insist they called me that throughout the date.

I bet you're sat there reading this thinking: it sounds pretty sweet being a lord. Well, yes, it is. But you can become a lord too, of course. Just buy the voucher on Groupon and redeem it at this website: www.scottishlaird.com. Go to the checkout to redeem your voucher. This is what it looks like:

You'll notice there's a bit in the menu for 'urgency'. You can make you order 'urgent'. Who needs to become a lord urgently? Who's that for? 'Hello, ScottishLairds.com? Yes,

I've told quite a substantial lie, I have a date in five hours, and I must be a lord by dusk!'

I was so excited to be a lord. Along with the Deeds to Dunans Castle I also received a letter from the caretaker of the estate, Mr Charles Dixon-Spain, cordially inviting me to visit Dunans Castle at my 'earliest possible convenience'. So they were clearly pretty excited to have me on board. Equally passionate about our nascent partnership, I decided to send my new Scottish friend this e-mail:

Dear Mr Dixon-Spain.

I am absolutely delighted to be Lord of Dunans Castle. As an Englishman, it is a tremendous honour and privilege for you to have me. I notice that I own around a square foot of the land on the estate. My research suggests that this amounts to a 12-inch by 12-inch plot of earth. And all that for 12 quid! That would cost me 200 grand in London. Anyway, here's the thing: would it be OK if I was buried in your grounds? I am not planning to die soon. This is not a suicide note. I would just like to make plans now for my own peace of mind. Whilst a square foot is not a huge amount of land, it would probably be sufficient if:

A) I was buried upright (like a statue)
B) I went on a diet
C) I had my legs and arms chopped off and cremated, with just my torso being buried. A sort of 'best-of-both' funeral, if you will. Which would please my parents who are absolutely clamouring for me to be burnt.

So what do you think? Dunans Castle has always been close to my heart since I bought the title last week, and it would mean a lot to me to rest for eternity amongst your glorious grounds. I won't be any bother. I certainly wouldn't haunt you. In fact, I think I would actually be quite a helpful ghost, keeping an eye out for poachers and the like.

I look forward to hearing from you.

Yours
Max Dickins

PS My favourite film is Braveheart.

And Mr Dixon-Spain replied!

Hi Max.

Great to hear from you. It's an unusual request, but one we have contemplated prior to your email. We do like the idea immensely, but at the moment we don't have any plans to accommodate burials – there are some restrictions in place we need to work out – but if and as we do, I will most certainly let you know!

Kind regards
Charles

Let's pick his message apart a little bit. Dodgy start, don't you think? 'Hi Max,' he says. Don't want to be a dick about it, but don't you think a lord deserves something a little more formal?

I'll give him the benefit of the doubt. Next up, Mr Dixon-Spain writes that my idea is: '... *an unusual request, but one we have contemplated prior to your email*'. What? HE'S BEEN THINKING ABOUT MY DEATH PRIOR TO MY EMAIL! What did he have planned? I was swiftly going off Mr Charles Dixon-Spain. Finally, the idea of strangers being buried in what is essentially his garden is one that he '*likes immensely*'. Who was this psychopath?

It seemed I could not visit my kingdom for fear of death. But it didn't mean that I couldn't still derive benefits from afar. And one of the reasons I purchased my title was that I expected it to open lots of doors for me. Literally. I literally expected people to open doors for me. As a nobleman I surely deserve more perks than you: a filthy peasant. So did I seek a membership to the Groucho Club? Attempt to be upgraded to business class on flights? Demand grazing rights in the City of London? No. I applied for a Nando's Black Card, which when I received it would entitle me to infinite free chicken for the rest of my life. I may have now been walking with kings, but I had not lost the common touch.

Nando's are a lot easier to get in touch with than you'd expect. You just have to go on their website and they provide a number of options for you to fire off your poultry missive. As they say: 'Whether you'd just like to say hello, or something wasn't quite right, we're always happy to hear from you.' This is a bit weird. What sort of maniac just wants to say 'Hello' to Nando's? '*Hello Nando's!*' Nando's is an abstract thing, not a human being. How lonely do you have to be to make small talk with a chicken shop? Also, what an utterly pointless thing to do. What are Nando's going to do in return? Become your pen-pal? Nando's offer a drop-down menu of options to select from when communicating with them. You can either say 'Something wasn't quite right' or 'Thanks so much'. I imagine 'Thanks so much' is not a popular option. Whose first thought after chicken and chips is to think 'I must e-mail head office'? The third and final option in the drop-down menu is: 'I have a great idea'. Notice it doesn't say, 'I have a great idea *for Nando's*'. Just 'I have a great idea'. And I did have a *brilliant* idea.

> *Hello Nando's! I'm Lord of Dunans Castle up in the Scottish Highlands. If you Google 'Dunans Castle' you'll see my house! Anyway, can I have a Black Card please? I promise to big you up to all the other lords and also to the royalty I'll inevitably end up hanging out with now. I promise not to lend it to any of my servants or prostitutes. Looking forward to hearing from you. If you're ever near the Scottish Highlands, do drop in for an Irn Brew. It would be peri-peri nice to meet you.*

Then I signed it off with the 'happy poo' emoji. And shiver me timbers, Nando's replied!

> *Hi Lord Max,*
>
> *Thanks for taking time out of your undoubtedly busy schedule to contact us.*
>
> *I'm sure you can appreciate when I say to you that I have absolutely no control over who gets a Nando's Black Card but if I did I would do my utmost best to try and get you one.*
> *Nevertheless it's brilliant to see how passionate you are about Nando's. I do enjoy a decent peri-peri meal*

myself if I must add.
Kindest regards,

Idris Allan
Customer Experience

What a shame! But at least it was brilliant for Idris to see how passionate I am about Nando's. I bet I made her day. In fact, when people ask me at job interviews or on dates what I am really passionate about, the first thing that comes to mind is: NANDO'S. It's all I think about, from the moment I get up to the moment I go to sleep. Nando's. Nando's. Nando's. But I'd reached a dead end on the Black Card front. Hopefully other perks would come my way soon. I shut my laptop and went to bed. The next morning I couldn't believe my luck. I stared at my inbox in disbelief, half expecting it to be a cruel hoax. My lord gambit had worked! I had managed to somehow land myself a date on Match.com as Lord Max Dickins. I was back in the dating game! Her name was Veronika, a redhead from the Ukraine with feisty eyes and lips you could sleep in. She was the *femme fatale* to my James Bond, if James Bond had eczema and an unhealthy obsession with discounts.

It was now up to me to plan our date. And luckily I lived with two girls who I could turn to for advice. 'You've got to do a Groupon!' said Philippa. Absolutely adamant, her face glowing in the light of a hundred candles. 'Definitely,' agreed Hope, who was chewing on a Rennie. 'You're the Groupon guy. She'll find it fun and interesting.' 'Absolutely,' said Phil, 'It will make up for your personality.' But I was unsure. In my limited experience it's often best to play it safe with first dates. I've learnt that the hard way: 'Paintballing-gate' was an absolute disaster. Although, to be fair, we did have a lovely picnic in A&E. But my flatmates were so convinced I should do a Groupon that they even bought a voucher for me. They wouldn't say what it was. They just gave me a postcode and told me it would be perfect. So I ran it past Veronika and she seemed to find the spontaneity romantic. Plus, I was a changed man now: I knew I could take anything in my stride. And so that was that. Our date was on.

We agreed to meet outside Holborn tube station. I stood nervously by the exit pretending to check e-mails on my phone. Five minutes later a woman in her fifties with terrible BO and what looked like beef mince on her cardigan approached me. 'Are you from Match.com?' she said. 'Oh you've got to be joking!' I thought. I know everyone presents a rose-tinted view of their looks on online dating profiles, but this was ridiculous. I thought about lying. There was still time to do a runner. But I panicked and spilt the beans. 'Yes I am,' I said. (I'd be such a rubbish spy). 'Great. Well ... ummm ... Hi! Gosh ... errr ... you look very different to your photo?' she said. Talk about the pot calling the kettle black. 'Yes. So do you,' I replied curtly. 'Well it's nice to meet you anyway, Ahmed,' she said. 'Oh thank God for that!' I roared. 'What do you mean?' she said. 'Oh! Sorry, I thought you were my date!' I said. 'But you're not so ... you know. That's brilliant.' 'Are you not Ahmed?' she said. 'No. Sorry. My name's Max.' 'Right. OK. Sorry.' She looked relieved too, actually. 'No worries. Hope you find him,' I said. She walked away, still covered in mince.

Another 10 minutes passed. Veronika was very late now. Convinced I'd been stood up, I was about to go home. 'Are you Lord Dickins?' I spun round and this time it really was her. She was beautiful. Even better than her photo. 'Oh please, call me Max,' I said, 'I don't stand on ceremony.' We shook hands and I pulled her into a slightly awkward hug. The date started well enough. Veronika was effervescent, giggling relentlessly. We got to know one another a bit. I told her I was a Londoner born and bred. She told me she grew up on a farm three hours north of Kiev. We talked about one another's hobbies: she was into rock climbing, and I was passionate about Nando's. I told her how to wrestle an alligator. She told me how to slaughter a cow. I'd forgotten how fun dating could be: I really liked this girl. We speculated wildly about what the waiting activity might be, before finally arriving at the anonymous venue. Veronika hadn't stop grinning yet, her celestial teeth glistening. Everything about her shone brightly and it was infectious. But her sunny disposition changed as soon as we walked through the front door. The Groupon was truly tragic.

A romantic couples photo shoot. Can you imagine a more awkward first date than that? Oh my, it was awful. Here are some of the shots:

I should emphasise that I have blurred out her face. That wasn't what her actual face looked like. She wasn't made out of Lego. No, I've had to blur out her face for legal reasons as – believe it or not – I haven't seen Veronika since. She never answered my calls and then soon left Match.com entirely. The whole date had lasted barely an hour. I arrived back home before nine o'clock. It was still light outside. My flatmates found the whole thing hilarious, of course. But I wasn't amused. 'Oh yes! Ha ha-ha! Thanks guys! Yeah, that's right! Take the piss out off the guy trying to mend a broken heart!' And to their credit they apologised. Philippa said, 'Look, we're really sorry. That was poor form; let us make it up to you. Let us buy you another Groupon that you'll actually enjoy.' And ever the nice guy, I said 'OK guys. I trust you.' And so later that evening they bought me a baby scan.

Chapter Eleven

Believe it or not, this was my first baby scan. I seriously considered not going. After all, it wasn't my money I'd be wasting. But the simple fact was that if I refused the call then I would lose the bet and incur The Groupon from Hell. (Although it was hard to see how it could be much worse than this.) So I called Dave and asked him to join me for some moral support, and off we went for my appointment on Harley Street. We entered the clinic and went up to the reception desk. 'Hello sir, how can I help you today?' said the girl, with Teflon friendliness. 'Oh hi, yes, my name's Max Dickins. I've got an appointment for a baby scan.' 'A baby scan, sir?' 'Yes that's right, a baby scan. This is my boyfriend, Dave.' Dave bit his lip. 'But you're a man, Mr Dickins?' 'Lord Dickins. I'm a Lord.' 'Right. OK. But you're a man, Lord Dickins.' 'Yes. Thank you. I am aware of that … well, it's just, we forgot to use protection the other day and we just want to make sure that … you know.' 'I see,' she said. 'The scan costs 80 pounds, Lord Dickins. You do realise that? It is non-refundable?' 'Yes, I know. But you can't put a price on peace of mind,' I said. 'And anyway: I've got this Groupon voucher …'

Dave and I sat in the waiting area, surrounded by heavily pregnant women leafing through glossy magazines and bored looking husbands who stared at us, totally baffled. A short time later a Latvian nurse with a clipboard came in and called my name. Sylvia led us upstairs into her airy consulting room. I lay down on the bed, pulled my shirt up beneath my chin, and she dispensed a large, cold dollop of transparent slime onto my belly. Sylvia was lovely, really putting me at ease at what was a very vulnerable time for me.

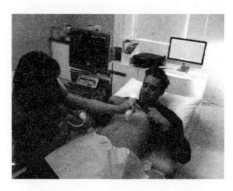

Having applied the lubricating gel, Sylvia then rubbed the ultrasound scanner on my tummy. Nothing was coming through on the screen. 'It looks like you're all clear,' said Sylvia, trying not to sound sarcastic. 'Phew,' said Dave, 'That's the last time we don't rubber up! Right, we better make a move, Max?' I wasn't satisfied though. 'I don't want to be difficult, Sylvia, but do you mind if I get a second opinion?' She looked like she wanted to slap me in the face. 'I'll have one last look,' she said, beginning to lube me up again.

And would you believe it! There he is: my son. He's due in October. I'm not sure who the father is, but my money's on Juan. This was another one of the scans:

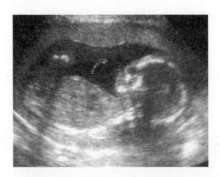

And if we zoom it close on that, you'll see a tiny plastic dolphin.

Sylvia wished me all the best but slowly herded Dave and me to the exit. 'Please take this complimentary CD of calming whale music,' she said, pushing it into my hand. 'It should help the baby sleep well.' 'Did you know that a whale's vagina is so big that you could walk around in it?' interjected Dave. Sylvia called security.

Later that evening, I told Philippa and Hope my good news. They were delighted that there would soon be a new tenant in the flat. We cracked open a bottle of cava to celebrate. It was rare that we were all in the building at the same time. After all, they both had proper 9–5 jobs, whereas I work mainly at night. So I found I was spending a lot of time by myself during the day. It's hard keeping up with your friends these days, isn't it? Everyone's so busy. I seem to spend my life texting my mates going: 'Do you want to go for a drink, mate? Do you want to go for a drink?' And they're always, like, 'No, I can't, I'm afraid, I'm having my breakfast'. Anyway, I realised I needed some new friends to hang out with in the daylight hours. So naturally I looked to Groupon for help. I saw this offer pop up:

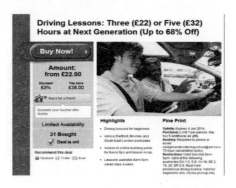

Three hours of driving lessons for just 22 quid. I bought it immediately. I could already drive, but I just fancied a bit of a chat with someone who was contractually obliged to listen. And it's fair to say the instructor was amazed at how good I was for a beginner. But I wasn't done yet, I also saw this come up:

And again I bought it. We didn't need anything fixing in the flat, but it was nice to have a blokey conversation for once. And there he is, Glenn:

He's changed his number now unfortunately. I also bought a voucher for eight weeks of swimming lessons. Again, I could already swim. In fact, I used to compete in galas for my school. I still hold the St Paul's School record for 'Jumping into the pool and rescuing a brick from the bottom whilst dressed in your pyjamas' competition. Or to give it it's official title 'Life Saving Bronze Award'. I went along to my first lesson and the instructor Lauren told me that I was the best novice she'd ever seen. She said that if I was ten years younger she thought I'd have a decent shot at becoming an Olympian. And I'll be honest, it felt good. But it was becoming clear that I was losing the plot. My obsession with Groupon had started off as charming and irreverent. Whenever I told people about my adventures they were impressed and inspired by my drive to self-improvement. Now when they found out what I'd been up to they just thought I was creepy.

Meanwhile I was still no closer to seducing Jen. The 'make her jealous' plan had failed miserably. I had continued to check my internet dating profile to see if my lordship credentials had helped me snare any more single beauties. But alas my inbox was empty. Not a dicky bird. Well, not quite. The woman who'd been covered in mince outside Holborn tube station had somehow found me and asked me out. But I wasn't taking Ahmed's sloppy seconds. So after almost a month as a nobleman I had come to the uncomfortable conclusion that becoming part of the landed aristocracy had frankly not changed my life in the way I had hoped. Becoming a lord simply hadn't been the magic bullet I'd assumed it would be. So I decided to raise the stakes and take my property empire intergalactic. I bought an acre of land on the planet Mars.

A week later, the prestigious sounding Lunar Embassy sent me a letter congratulating me on my exclusive purchase. They also included a map showing me which specific plot I now owned. I was future-proofed. Come the inevitable apocalypse I now had somewhere to escape to. But before finding it on Groupon, I was unaware that space was even up for sale. Google swiftly informed me, however, that an American called Dennis Hope owns it. Dennis claims to have found a loophole in the only internationally recognised law relating to the ownership of extraterrestrial property: the Outer Space Treaty of 1967. He filed his claim with the United Nations on 22nd November 1980. Article 2 of The Outer Space Treaty states that *'no nation by appropriation shall have sovereignty or control over any of the satellite bodies'*. In short, no countries can own space.

However, Hope's argument is that nowhere in the treaty does it mention individuals can't do that, though. So he sent a note to the UN saying that if they had a legal problem with his claim of ownership of the entire contents of space to let him know. They didn't do anything. Perhaps they were busy with a war or a genocide or something. He has never heard back from them and so naturally assumes that they are absolutely fine with the whole idea. It's amazing logic from Dennis. And an argument I began using in my own life. For example, I tweeted the pop star Rihanna telling her that she was my girlfriend. She never got back to me, ergo, I am Rihanna's boyfriend.

Tweets

Max Dickins @maxdickins
Hey @rihanna just to let you know: you are my girlfriend now. I assume this is cool. I am happy to do this long distance–we're both busy.
Expand   ↶ Reply   🗑 Delete   ★ Favorite   ••• More

Groupon had offered me the choice between buying an acre of land on either Mars, Venus, or the Moon. It was a tough decision. The Moon is the closest, but I thought: would I want to spend any length of time on a barren landscape that can barely support living organisms, let alone essential retail and even the most basic cultural space? I mean, I've been to Swindon before and I didn't enjoy it. Venus was a tempting option too, as it's famously crammed full of women. But in the end I plumped for Mars as scientists think it's the most liveable and a potential destination for human expansion, so property prices could skyrocket. In fact, if the current rates of urban sprawl continue, Mars may count as Greater London by 2050. Mars is 250 million miles away from Earth, or to put it in estate agent's terms 'easily commutable'. It's also quiet and roomy, with great views of the abyss.

My gift-pack contained a 'Martian Constitution', which was essentially the Bill of Rights for the Planet Mars. Some of the contents were alarming. For example, it said that Mars will be ruled by 'The Big Cheese' (Dennis Hope) for all eternity. The Big Cheese will be 'totally omnipotent' and will make changes to the constitution 'as needed to fulfil the pursuit of happiness and bigger profits'. In the other words, Dennis Hope has free reign to do whatever he fancies. He could paint a giant cock and balls on the side of it if he wants. This is what happens when an American invades space. I was furious. But my letter of congratulations from the Lunar Embassy foolishly ended with the sentence: 'If you would like to give us some feedback or ask any questions, we're always happy to hear from you. Please e-mail: info@moonestates.com'. That was like a red-rag to a bull. So I dropped Dennis a line.

Dear Mr Big Cheese.

I was incredibly excited to purchase an acre of land on the planet Mars. Space has always been a massive passion of mine. (Indeed I think I may have actually been abducted by aliens in 2010, although I was doing a lot of MDMA at the time.) So you can imagine how chuffed I was to have bought my very own plot on the Red Planet.

However, I was worried to read your Martian Constitution. You seem to have total disdain for democracy. I take my right to vote very seriously (I have voted in every X Factor final in history). So as you can imagine, as a fan of democracy, that to have recently bought a plot of land on your sinister dictatorship has left me feeling like a Bulgarian who has checked into a B&B, only to find out it's managed by Nigel Farage.

How do you defend your constitution? After all, you are from America, the country that invented freedom. Throughout history the United States has always stood up for democracy. Without American freedom fighters the whole world would be ruled by Nazi Muslims. And no one wants that. (Not even Nazis – they hated Muslims). Is your heritage not worth protecting?

Yours
Lord Max Dickins (one of your Mini Cheddars)

PS. Would it be possible to be buried on Mars? This is not a suicide note, I am not planning to die soon. I would just like to get my affairs in order for my own peace of mind.

PPS. Will there be a Nando's on Mars?

I never received a reply. Maybe it's in Dennis Hope's spam folder? It's crucial to check your spam folder, otherwise you might miss something very important. After all, the UN forgot to check theirs and ended up giving away the whole of space. I looked at mine the other day and it turned out that I'd won the Nigerian lottery on 12 separate occasions! What are the odds? And I'd missed the boat every single time. Just my luck. But even though I seemed impotent in reforming the Martian Constitution, what could not be denied was that I was now quite the catch – an alligator wrestling Lord of the Realm with an intergalactic property portfolio. I may have been losing my mind, but I was also gaining sex appeal. It was surely only a matter of time before someone would bite. But it was now just eight weeks until my cousin's wedding. So I needed a result fast.

Chapter Twelve

'Oh sweet mother of Christ it's her!' My stomach lurched and I froze as she walked towards me. She didn't recognise me straight away. So I concentrated on looking like I hadn't seen her either. I fiddled with my phone and affected frustration about the long wait for the toilet. 'Wow ... Max. Is that ... Hi?' God, she looked gorgeous. It was late June. I hadn't seen Jen since November. And now, totally randomly, here she was. A bonfire of beauty. Stood right there in front of me at a house party in Brixton. I had thought about this moment of reunion a million times. I'd thought about what I'd say. What pithy, funny, cool one-liner I'd crack. Now was my chance to bring it out and make her heart skip a beat. 'I didn't follow you here,' I said. This was admittedly not the best opening gambit in the history of conversations. Luckily, Jen laughed. Wrongly assuming that I was being deliberately humorous. 'Well. That's a relief!' she said. I continued to stare at her, unwilling to risk another sentence. 'So ... ummm ... what's new with you?' she said eventually. And suddenly I found my voice: I told her *everything*.

'I'm totally spontaneous these days, you know? Yeah, yeah, yeah ... I wouldn't use the word *massive legend* but ...' Jen frowned, 'That's two words?' 'What? Oh. Right. Yes. I see. All I'm trying to say Jen, is that my life is MAD now! I've gone absolutely mental!' 'Yes, I'd heard that actually,' she said. 'Look, I know someone who might be able to help?' 'What? No, I'm not actually mental. Not literally. I'm just … I'm just having loads of fun, that's all.' 'Great,' she said, 'I'm glad.' 'Yes. Great,' I said. 'Well, I better go and find my friends,' she said, 'I'll see you later though, yeah? Maybe you can do some of your hilarious dancing!' 'What hilarious dancing?' I said. But she had already begun to walk away.

'We should do a Groupon together!' I cried after her, a little too loudly. She stopped in her tracks and turned to look at me again. 'Why don't you come clay pigeon shooting with me next Saturday?' Jen was stunned. This sort of boldness, this *carpe*-ing of the *diem*, was something she'd never seen from me before. I surprised myself to tell you the truth. But I'd learnt a lot from the alligator wrestling: don't hesitate, don't let go. Jen laughed again and then bit her bottom lip. 'Max … wow … I don't …' She trailed off into silence, leaving me marooned in the acidic uncertainty of my rash offer. Jen had my heart in her hands once more. I had humiliated myself. I knew it. In front of all these people too. The eight strong queue for the toilet was now staring at me, as my face turned rose red. God, I felt like such an idiot. *Why do I always do this to myself? Why can't I just be normal?*

'Yeah, OK then,' she said, 'Why not? Sounds fun.' 'Ummm … sorry what?' I said. I was not expecting this. 'I'm saying yes, Max. I'd like to go clay pigeon shooting with you.' 'Oh! Right. Nice. Well … I'll text you about it. Cool?' I was feigning indifference but I felt like jumping around. 'But only as friends, yeah?' she said. 'Sure. Yeah, just as friends. Obviously. God yeah! Blimey!' I said. But I didn't mean it. Because we all know what people mean when they say 'just as friends'. It's a figure of speech, a turn of phrase. 'Friends' is just a polite way of saying 'turbocharged boning squads'. So, I now had a week to get in the best possible shape for a clay pigeon shooting date with my ex-girlfriend.

Our relationship was back on again. I would have to let Rihanna down gently.

The next day I called an emergency house meeting. Hope and Philippa gathered in the living room. They looked concerned. 'God, you're not coming out, are you?' asked Philippa. 'If you've eaten my Parma ham again I'm going to neuter you with my hair straighteners,' said Hope. 'I told you to stop buying it!' I said. 'I can't help myself!' 'You can help yourself,' said Hope, 'that's the problem.' I apologised again and explained the real reason for calling the meeting. 'I just need some advice,' I said. 'Is this going to take long?' said Hope, whose moustache was covered in a thick layer of hair removal cream. 'It's just I need to wipe this off soon otherwise it will burn.' 'It will take two minutes,' I said. Hope nodded reluctantly. 'OK, so I bumped into Jen at a house party last night,' I said. 'Go on,' said Philippa. 'Oh God, you didn't do any of your funny dancing, did you?' added Hope. 'What funny dancing?' I said. 'Don't worry about it,' she said.

'Basically I need a female perspective. I'm going on a date with her on Saturday. This is my last chance, I think. It has to go well otherwise, that's it: I might lose the love of my life forever. So what do I have to do?' The girls looked at each other for a moment. 'You've got to make her jealous. You've got to make her think that she lost something amazing when she dumped you,' said Phil. 'I agree,' said Hope, 'but you can put lipstick on a pig, and it's still a pig.' 'OK. That's great, thank you,' I said, 'but what exactly should I do?' 'You've got to look GREAT,' said Phil. 'Well, as good as you can, at least ...' added Hope. 'Get a spray tan,' said Phil. 'A spray tan?' I said. 'Are you sure I won't look like a massive twat?' 'Of course not,' said Hope, 'everyone looks great with a tan!' 'Can you spray tan a pig?' pondered Phil. 'Not easily,' said Hope, 'but once, on my gap year ...' 'Guys, can you stop saying I'm a pig?' I said.

And so, for want of better judgement, that afternoon I went off to The Tanning Salon in Clapham to have a spray tan. An hour later I was stood in the lobby at the salon. On the way in I walked past a middle-aged woman the colour of an orangutan's ball bag. She was a deep Lucozade orange, like a sub-Saharan reptile, or a Geordie. I approached the reception desk. Waiting there was Kayleigh in her skimpy black uniform, like a chorizo wrapped in a napkin. 'Hello sir, I'm Kayleigh. What colour would you like? "Dark" or "Dark-dark"?' she said. 'I don't know what you mean by that, Kayleigh. What's the difference?' 'Well, do you want to look like Enrique Iglesias or Denzel Washington?' she said. I thought about it for a second and then decided to play it safe. I went for 'Dark'. Next I was shown to an electronic spray tanning booth. Kayleigh was very cheerful, giggling away as we walked down the stairs and asking me lots of questions, including: 'So are you having this for a special occasion or is it just a treat for your boyfriend?'

In the cubicle an electronic woman's voice talked me through the whole process. All I had to do was strip totally naked and put a blue fishnet cap on my head. So by the time I stepped into the booth I looked like a Greggs's employee who'd had a breakdown. Then the spraying began: the nozzles ejecting microscopic beads of brown paint in a cold mist. It's a very weird smell, spray tan. It's like a cross between chocolate and low self-esteem. I got out of the booth and looked at myself in the full-length mirror. I didn't look *that* brown. So I went upstairs to protest. Kayleigh tried to put me at ease. 'Actually sir, you're going to get really dark in, like, eight hours' time.' And in eight hours' time I was at the Bloomsbury Theatre in London, watching a show. There were three intervals in this show, and each time I came back from the interval I was a different race of human. To the point where I came back from the third interval, and the bloke sitting next to me just went, 'Errr, sorry, someone's sitting there, mate,' and I was like, 'No, no, no, it's just me. I'm blacked up.' Here's a photo of me the next day:

The following morning a parcel dropped on the doormat. I'd promised myself that I would leave no stone unturned in my quest to win Jen back. I would be primped, preened and pristine for our date. I wanted her to look at me and swoon. So when I'd seen an ab toning belt pop up on Groupon it was a no-brainer. It's the sort of gimmick that you see advertised on Eurosport in the middle of the night when they've run out of skiing to show. You've seen the adverts. Most of them are American. They tend to come in two broad categories. Firstly you have the JML ads, flogging various gizmos that promise to reinvent homeware in ways that you'll never need. Like a bin that can sing. Or a kettle that runs on farts. Or a walk-in oven.

Then you have the fitness equipment commercials. Terracotta gods, stomachs like vacuum-packed soap, telling you that you can have it all: a great bod, zero exercise. They show 'before' photos of dumpy Americans. They're wearing baggy polyester clothes and barely have faces, so they look like a thumb in a maternity gown. Then they show an 'after' photo – newly chiselled features glow back at you. Their life has been completely transformed. They aren't obese anymore, they've got a tan now, and they've taken up salsa. (The dance I mean, not the dip.) They look down the barrel of the camera and tell pathetic old you, slumped on the sofa cupping your clammy testicles, can of beer in hand: 'If you use this toning belt for *JUST 20 MINUTES* a day, then you can have the body you always dreamed of'. It's so tempting.

I ripped the belt from its plastic womb and tried it for size. It was a rectangular elastic waistband with a small red computer box on the front, dotted with rubber buttons. There were four different settings. I've got no idea what they did. I didn't read the instructions, obviously. No one ever does. There could have been a photo of the manufacturer executing a dolphin on page five for all I know. Spiky jabs of electricity pulsed through my stomach muscles. The sensation was one of butterflies, of feeling nervous, of the ominous tumbling of bowels. That evening I had my first proper workout. I sat watching *Countryfile* with a glass of red wine and some crumpets, toning belt on. I did 20 minutes on level two. But because in life you get back what you put in, I poured myself another glass of wine and did another 20 minutes. I live for the burn. The next evening I flopped down in front of the Women's Darts World Championships on Eurosport, with a ready meal, and did a full hour. What can I say? I'm goal orientated.

After such a strenuous workout it was important that I warmed down properly. So I had a bath. Then I downed a protein shake (is lager a protein?) and went to bed. But not before going online and placing a Groupon order for some vibrating buttock pads. Boy, did I sleep well that night. But I awoke the next day to some bad news. The girls had scoured Groupon too and consequently booked me an afternoon appointment with a stylist. On the surface, this seemed to be another giant leap towards my ultimate goal of looking hot for my ex-girlfriend. But that didn't mean I wasn't dreading it. Before I moved in to the flat I always thought I'd dressed rather well. I suppose everyone thinks they've got style. Nobody looks in the mirror before they leave the house and thinks, 'Well, I look like a total arsehole. Anyway, off to work'. No, they see their clothes reflected back to them and feel at least a small sense of satisfaction. However Hope and Philippa had since taken to nicknaming me 'Dad', on the basis of not just my dancing but also my propensity to dress like Jeremy Clarkson. So, sat on the tube on the way to my rendezvous with the stylist, I was wary of a backlash.

Her name was Trudy. She had enough Botox in her face to disable a *Tyrannosaurus rex*, and was dressed like a Parisian *dominatrix*. I rolled up in the clothes I'd been wearing all day. I'd thought about changing into my best gear but I wanted to hear the honest, unvarnished truth. And I certainly got it. It turns out that I am to fashion what Edward Scissorhands is to masturbation. 'What's with the horrible man bag? And did your grandad die in those jeans? Oh, and Jesus called: he wants his sandals back', she said, totally baffled. I say baffled – it was impossible to tell. But I wasn't going to go down without a fight. 'Surely there are more important things in the world than how we dress? Yeah? Like war? Or famine? Surely these are the goals humanity should be investing its energy in? So forgive me for not giving a toss about fashion, I'm too busy thinking about the starving Africans.' Trudy looked at me with a mixture of pity and fury. 'Look, Max, do you want to get a shag or not?'

(*Touché*). She removed my trilby hat and put it straight in the bin.

'Trudy, I think it's time you paid me a bit more respect actually. I am a lord you know?' I said. 'I'm just doing my job,' she said. 'That's what the Nazi war criminals said,' I snapped. 'So you think I dress badly?' 'No, I don't actually,' she said. 'I think it's a lot worse than that.' 'Yeah, but that's just your opinion,' I said. 'I bet there are tons of other people who actually love my clothes.' I was fired up. 'Alright then,' she said, 'let's see.' Trudy stopped a passer-by in the street. A beautiful Norwegian girl called Pernilla. She asked her how old she thought I was. 'I would say he looks about 37,' she said. 'Tell her how old you are, Max.' 'Hi Pernilla. I'm actually 26.' 'I'm so sorry,' she said. 'Oh don't apologise,' I said, 'I'm not offended.' 'No, I mean, I'm just … sorry.'

Defeated and demoralised, I followed Trudy into the throbbing shops. She proceeded to load me up with a plethora of fashionable garments. It was like a really camp game of *Buckaroo!* 'Denim is your best friend,' she said, lobbing some skinny jeans at me. We spent two hours traipsing up and down Oxford Street. My credit card debt growing more and more extortionate with each new doorway. Trudy told me that it was important to accessorise. 'Watches are timeless,' she said. 'No. I think your watch must be broken,' I said. She didn't laugh. But to be fair I don't think she was able to. Her cheeks were far too taut. The only way to decipher any emotional response from Trudy was to look deep into her eyes. Everything else remained entirely still. She was like one of those portrait paintings where the eyes have been scoured out and replaced with peepholes. After three hours of shopping we finally took a timeout. Trudy had a wheatgrass shot and I had a McFlurry. 'Do you know what the secret to my youthful complexion is, Max?' she asked.

'No idea,' I said, although I obviously did. 'Sperm,' she said. This wasn't the answer I was expecting. 'I rub it on my face every evening.' I immediately put my McFlurry in the bin.

At the end of our retail odyssey, Trudy wished me luck with my looming date and presented her hand for me to kiss, which I did reluctantly, aware of what she'd been using them for. I returned to the flat that evening hunched over by eight bags of brand new clobber, convex but content. Philippa and Hope were very excited by my haul, and insisted I do a full fashion show for them immediately. My self-conscious struts up and down the living room were met with gasps of approval. 'Much, much better,' said Philippa. 'Definitely,' agreed Hope. 'You no longer look like you're terminally ill and on a final trip to Alton Towers.' I was beginning to feel much more confident about myself. Then Hope spoke again, 'All we have to do now is pluck your monobrow.' Ten minutes later I was tanned, toned, trendy and tweezered. I was ready to go shooting with my ex-girlfriend. And the very next day, that's exactly what I did.

Chapter Thirteen

I picked Jen up outside her flat. The flat that had seen the best and the worst of our love. The whispered odes, the hatched plans, the 'ok' sex (not my words). But also the passive-aggressive silences, the tears, the doubts. I got there far too early, so I parked around the corner and listened to the whale music CD to try and keep calm. I opened a window. It was a balmy day and I didn't want to sweat in case my spray tan started to run. Twenty minutes later she was in my car. We kissed each other on the cheek. 'It's great to see you,' she said. Jen looked beautiful, but she always does. Shards of light burst out of every pore. Her long, blonde hair a gleaming road to a better place. The arch of her neck sloping down to her shoulders, the prologue to a book I longed to read again. 'Is that tan real?' she asked. 'Yeah, of course!' I said. She nodded, unconvinced. 'You've got a new look?' she said. 'Have I?' I said. 'I just threw this on to be honest.' We set off down the M4 towards the Oxfordshire countryside. I wouldn't normally go the countryside. I find it boring. The only good thing about the countryside is cows. I bloody love cows; I could watch them for hours. But cows become really sad if you imagine that '*moo*' translates as '*help*'.

We stopped off at a local gastro pub for lunch. 'What the hell are triple-cooked chips?' Jen was glaring at the menu, furious. 'Why does every aspect of every single bloody dish have to be described with an unnecessary and meaningless adjective?' Jen was on the rampage and I was finding her sexier and sexier. There are two sure ways to my heart: a passion for food, and angry pedantry. She was nailing both. 'And they've described the bread as "oven-baked". How else are you supposed to make bread? In the kettle?' The waiter came over to take our order. I sensed an opportunity to do one of my trademark riffs. 'Hey mate, what's the deal with triple cooked chips?! I don't think I've ever come back from a restaurant and said "*It was OK, I suppose … but I can't believe they only cooked the chips once*".' Jen nodded cheerfully. I was smashing it out of the park. This is what she'd been missing in the intervening months since our break-up: a sounding board for chip-based fury.

The waiter smiled politely at my hilarious joke. 'Actually the chips are triple-cooked because it makes them crispy,' he explained. 'Fair enough. But I don't see why I need to read the biography of every ingredient in every dish. I want to eat it, not date it!' Jen had stopped smiling now, but I was on a roll. 'Like, who cares where the parsnips went to school right?!' OK, I'd taken it too far. I'd lost the room. Jen was staring out of the window, waiting for me to finish with an embarrassed look on her face. The waiter just looked bored. 'I'll come back in a minute,' he said.

Lunch was delicious. I had smoked salmon. Or '*oak-smoked finest organic Scottish salmon from the choppy, melancholic waters of the Outer Hebrides, cured with the tears of a Highland widow*'. Jen had '*gay haddock*'. We chatted effortlessly. It was just like old times. During dessert I put my hand on top of hers. She didn't take it off. After lunch we got back in the car and drove through acres of farmland, down a long dirt track road towards the shooting lodge. We parked up beside a shed full of cows, who were mooing like mad/begging for help. Inside the small wooden hut waited Frank. Stooped over in a green Barbour and wellies, he had nose hair that could trap a helicopter, and wild grey eyebrows like a Thunderbird. They looked as if they might turn into butterflies and fly off any minute. I was stood there with my refulgent orange spray tan and the extravagant garb Trudy had put me in. Frank just gawped, flabbergasted. It looked like Liberace had walked onto the set of *Midsomer Murders*. He finally spoke: 'My wife's got one of them scarfs!' Frank lost his mind at how funny this was. I could hear the snap, crackle and pop of my ex-girlfriend's ovaries drying up. Luckily two other people had now arrived: a father and his teenage son, both of them in full camouflage gear. This was not explained.

It was finally time to go out and shoot. Here was my chance to prove to Jen and to Frank that I was a real man. I was pumped up. Frank handed me a shotgun. I held the girthy weapon in my hands and visualised the glory that was soon to be mine. The gun was heavy, about nine kilos, which is equivalent to three small cats. The Clay pigeons are fired out of the traps, eight at a time, so that they fly through the air in the manner of real birds. You then shoot them out of the sky. Frank explained the technique. You put the wooden butt of the gun into the groove between your neck and your shoulder, hold the barrel against your cheekbone with your left hand, and pull the trigger with your right. Easy-peasy. We've all seen films: civilians in siege situations picking up guns willy-nilly and being able to use them no problem. I'd be fine. I'd had a dry run in Texas anyway. Piece of cake.

'Right, who's up first?' asked Frank. I stepped forward assertively. 'Do you remember what I said?' he asked. 'Yes,' I said, despite the fact I hadn't listened to a word of it, but had instead hummed the *Top Gun* theme tune whilst fantasising about shooting terrorists in the dick. Frank loaded up the barrel with cartridges. 'Right then, let's be having you.' It was my time to shine. I winked at Jen and took my position. To be honest I looked less like a deadly marksman and more like a maniac about to go on the rampage in Top Man. I took a deep breath. And began. BANG! BANG! BANG! BANG! BANG! BANG! BANG! BANG! I missed eight out of eight.

Frank was staggered by how bad I was, shaking his head in befuddled amusement. 'Bloody hell, Stevie Wonder!' he said. 'What the hell are you aiming at?' He then pretended to be cross-eyed for a bit. Classic banter from Frank. I laughed to show I was a good sport. Everyone else laughed too. He reloaded the gun and I had another go. Exactly the same thing happened. Frank said, 'Someone asked me the other day "Has there ever been anyone you couldn't teach how to shoot?" And I said "no." But now I've met you.' I laughed again, but this time for far too long and far too loud, so that it was obvious I was faking it. Jen smiled uncomfortably.

I'd be a really crap hitman. If it was me who tried to knock off JFK he'd still be alive today. I'd have just accidentally shot an ice cream man 40 feet to his left, in the most baffling assassination of all time. I was terrible at shooting but Jen was brilliant, which Frank thought was hilarious. 'Even a woman's better than you!' Oh yes Frank! How funny! Imagine that? A woman with skills! What next? Fire? Still, I was embarrassed at my ineptitude. But it wasn't the end of the world. The fact was that I'd shown to Jen even by being here that I'd changed. In the car on the way home we discussed all my other adventures. I regaled her with tales of taming alligators, punching women at Gong Baths, and jet washing my intestines. By now we were coming off the M4 into Hammersmith. 'Shall I drop you back at the flat?' I said. 'Actually, if it's not too much of a pain, do you mind dropping me in Surbiton?' she said. 'Yeah sure. No worries. You meeting a friend or something?' I said. 'No. It's just … well … I'm staying with my boyfriend tonight.' Wallop.

This was devastating news. It was definitely over. I had deluded myself. My heart had tricked my head; hope had won a cruel victory over dignity. My face started to burn. I could feel myself turning crimson. 'You didn't think this was a date, did you?' said Jen. 'I did say …' I couldn't speak. I had no words. I concentrated on not bursting into tears. I felt like such an idiot. She'd moved on, of course she had. Why shouldn't she? We were over, and we had been for months. In hindsight, it was so obvious and yet I'd just totally embarrassed myself trying to impress her. Trying to look manly with a gun; turning up with a spray tan. Like some sort of Umpa Lumpa Vladimir Putin.

I dropped her off. He lived in a lovely area, the bastard. His wheelie bin was brand new and absolutely massive. This guy was clearly a player. Jen and I shared another awkward kiss. This time I left an orange smear across her right cheek. I didn't have the strength to tell her, though: I'd been humiliated enough already. It was getting dark now but I could see him stood in the window of his second floor flat, silhouetted in the light of the living room. He looked tall and muscular. He's so masculine he probably ejaculates hammers, I thought. One thing's for sure, he could definitely shoot the living shit out of a clay pigeon. Then he'd march over to the shattered ceramic shards and chew them as if they were marshmallows. 'I had a really lovely time,' she said before getting out. This was scant comfort. I drove off as Jen put the key into the door. Out of sight of her pitying eyes and his powerful arms, I broke down. (Emotionally, I mean. The car was fine.) Not even the mournful yawns of the whales could dam my tears. I knew now that I'd reached the end of the road. (Literally: he lived in a cul-de-sac.)

My Groupon Adventure had been a pointless waste of time. I began with a simple goal: to win Jen back, and I had failed. I'd invested a huge amount of time, energy and money into this project. And what did I have to show for it? A huge debt, a worthless lordship, and an album of creepy photos from a disastrous first date. All I had left was Groupon. The only consolation was that I was on target to win my bet with Dave. I had forged this identity as a spontaneous drifter, an intrepid explorer blazing a trail of adventure. That was the true legacy of these past seven months. And I would hold on to it for dear life, like a doomed soldier in a war zone, clinging onto the crumpled black and white photo of a loved one. But unlike the photo, which might spur on the soldier to acts of bravery and defiance, this crazy identity of mine contained the blueprint for my own destruction. I had nothing to lose anymore except my belief in the power of adventure. And little did I know that it was this very belief that would cause my life to totally unravel.

Chapter Fourteen

I needed a holiday. My heart had just been broken all over again and I had to get away somewhere quiet to lick my wounds. I wanted to go on a minibreak. The trouble is, it's very hard to go on holiday as a single man. If you ask your female mates if they'd like to join you on holiday they find it weird. They see it as always tinged with romantic undertones. Like a desperate yelp from deep within the shadows of the friend zone. And likewise if you ask a male friend if they'd like to come on holiday with you it makes them really uncomfortable. This is a male problem; straight women going on breaks with other straight women is considered totally normal. Nobody bats an eyelid. But vice versa it's a no-no: male-on-male minibreaks are the last taboo. Men can go on holiday with other men, but only if it's in a group. That's 'lads on tour'. A friend of mine was showing me video on his mobile phone from a holiday to the Algarve he'd recently returned from, with some 'rugby lads'. It was a video of them all wrestling on the beach, totally naked, covered in lube. He then asked me if I had a holiday planned. I said, 'I might go to Dublin with my mate Mark.' He looked at me and said, 'That's a bit gay, mate.'

Why are men so reluctant to go on holiday with other men? Perhaps it's because they fear being assumed homosexual? Even if they're not homophobic, there's a subconscious unease about being thought gay. This is probably a legacy of the stigma attached to being a gay man historically, which was a lot stronger than it was towards gay women. Mainly, I think, because a lot of people didn't think that lesbians were real. They put them in the same category as unicorns. This is still the case for a lot of people. I told my gran that a friend of mine recently came out as a lesbian and she was absolutely baffled. She refused to believe they even existed. So I had to show her a video.

However, I was unperturbed. I was going on a minibreak and if I had to go alone then so be it. Dave had already turned me down, he was busy with a 'secret project', which he said he couldn't talk about yet. But Groupon was my saviour. I scrolled down to the 'Getaways' section on their website. One offer in particular caught my eye: '70% off: four-day minibreak in the beautiful Lake District'. I bought it straight off the bat. It was a B&B in the sleepy Cumbrian town of Kendal. The accommodation was described as 'characterful', which was ominous. In the hospitality business 'characterful' is a synonym for 'dilapidated'. Just like when my parents tell me a friend of theirs is 'a bit of a character' they actually mean 'conversationally racist'. A characterful B&B simply meant that there would be blood in the shower and the proprietor would be a cyclops.

In the end, I was pleasantly surprised. The B&B was actually fine. After an eight-hour trip North, I dumped my bags and lay on the bed contemplating what I should do that evening. The world was my oyster. I could do absolutely anything I pleased. Yes Kendal was a pretty comatose town, so maybe the world was my clam. But I was a travelling bohemian with the world at my feet. No one to tie me down. I could write poetry overlooking the Fells like Wordsworth! I could swim naked in a brook! I could contemplate the meaning of the universe whilst staring up at the stars! In the end I went to the pub. I sought out a quiet corner and began to read a book. What could go wrong?

If you go to a pub alone you become a magnet to the 'characters': the lonely regulars with their darting, bloodshot eyes. They know you have no escape strategy, no reasonable excuse not to talk to them. After all, you've come to the pub alone. It took only five minutes for the first madman to seek me out. He was bald and pot-bellied with pasty, tattooed arms. His teeth looked like he'd been using them to tow frigates. 'How do? I'm Gary. I suppose you want some company?' he said – incorrectly. I smiled politely. 'Reading a book are yer? Well lah-di-da,' he continued, as if I'd come in here deliberately to taunt him. 'I'm Max,' I said. 'Hello, Max,' he said, picking up my hand and shaking it. 'And what brings you to Kendal?' I didn't want to say I was on holiday alone. That was far too embarrassing. So instead I told him I was a travelling Jehovah's Witness. I thought that might put him off. Then I remembered I was reading a book called *The God Delusion* by Richard Dawkins.

Luckily Gary didn't notice. He was much more interested in telling me his entire life story. 'I'm a businessman me. Don't get me wrong: I'm a working class lad but I've done alright for myself,' he said. 'I've got three A-levels. After school I wasn't sure what to do with my life. So my dad sat me down, and he told me that no one from our family had ever been to university and it was about time someone took that leap. So he enrolled at Leeds Met and I had to become the breadwinner.' I laboured a thin smile and looked at my glass. I still had three-quarters of a pint left so I'd have to sit this out a while yet. 'I do self-defence training classes. I could teach you to kill a man in one punch,' he said. I bet Jen's new boyfriend can kill a man with one punch, I thought. Or with just one icy blue stare of his heavenly eyes.

'I've built this business up from nothing,' continued Gary, unperturbed by the rank ambivalence written across my face. 'I've never had any help; no bank would lend me money. I went on that *Dragons' Den* a couple of year ago. But I was thrown off after I accidentally broke Deborah Meaden's arm.' I now had half a pint left. 'I understand the psychology of violence, you see,' said Gary, holding court. 'A violent criminal will attack the weak; he's looking for signs of weakness. So once you see signals of aggression you must strike before they strike you. The best form of self-defence in my view is premeditated violence.'

I offered Gary a crisp. 'No thanks, mate. Best not. You've got to be fit in my game. I get up at 6am every morning and go for an eight-mile run. Then it's back home for breakfast. I have six eggs for protein, not the yolks though: they're full of calories. And then nine or ten sausages. And a cake, to get my blood sugar up.' I downed the rest of my pint. 'I've got to go, Gary, I'm afraid,' I said, already putting on my coat. 'Have you ever killed a man, Max?' he said, stopping me in my tracks. 'Sorry?' I said. 'Have you ever killed a man?' 'No. Can't say I have. Errr … have you?' 'Yep. Oh yes.' I stared at him open-mouthed. 'What happened?' I said. 'It was food poisoning. I were working in Little Chef at the time. But it still counts. Let me get you another pint.'

Five pints later, Gary hadn't drawn breath. We'd now been joined by Phil, who worked as a security worker for concert promoter Live Nation. Phil was spellbound by Gary and his spiel. Gary eventually suggested that Phil could use his terrifying techniques in his security work. 'Oh definitely. I do big festivals, backstage mainly. But it's not the punters you want to watch out for, it's the bloody pop stars!' 'Really?' I said, now quite pissed. 'Like I did Download Festival a couple of weeks back. I'm backstage and these blokes just try and walk past me. I'm like, "Whoa, whoa, whoa fellas! Where do you think you're going?" They said, "We're The Prodigy. We're due on stage right now." And I'm like, "Do you think I were born yesterday lads! The Prodigy my arse!" I didn't let them past. They start going fucking mental. "WE'RE THE FUCKING PRODIGY!" they were screaming. "WE'RE FUCKING HEADLINING!" And I said, "Where's your passes, lads?" They pointed at a poster. They said, "That's us there." I said, "How do I know you're not lookalikes?" 'Cos they had an Elvis impersonator at my brother's wedding and he were an absolute spit. Anyway, they stormed off and they never came back. One-nil, Phil.' 'Was it The Prodigy?' I said. 'In hindsight, it was, yeah. They cancelled the gig and the crowd rioted. But rules is rules.'

I went to the toilet. When I returned the pair were stood up in the middle of the pub so Gary could do a demonstration. 'Right, Phil, grab my shirt with your right hand, up on my left shoulder.' Phil did as he was told. 'Now this is a common attack you might face. The self-defence move here is clear: I would just smash my right palm straight into your nose. Just like this. Bang!' Phil was now prostrate on the floor with a broken nose, mewling in great pain. This was my opportunity to make an escape, and I bolted for the door. Back in my double room at the B&B the landlady had left out two bath robes and two pairs of slippers. She really didn't know me at all. Then I looked at my bedside table and saw an enormous box of tissues and realised that maybe she knew me a lot better than I thought. The sight of the dressing gowns and slippers made me feel achingly lonely. I put one set on and stared at the other longingly. Jen loved a dressing gown. Unable to look at the spare robe any longer I put that one on too and set about planning my itinerary for the next day. Twenty minutes later I was incredibly sweaty but ready for bed.

The Lake District lives up to the hype. Abundant drystone walls the grey membranes on a patchwork of ecstatic greens. Everywhere these pockets of life glow – green alveoli in lungs blowing oxygen straight into the human heart. All the while shivering trees sprout wildly like carbuncles on the swollen hills. William Wordsworth described it best of course, and I would visit his old home Dove Cottage later that afternoon. First on the menu though was Beatrix Potter's Hill Top Farm. I came here because it reminded me of my childhood. How I longed for that simplicity now. Potter is most famous for her Peter Rabbit books. But she also wrote *The Tale of Squirrel Nutkin*, and an erotic novel called *The Filthy Billionaire*. (Although I'm suspicious that Wikipedia has not got this last fact entirely correct.) She donated Hill Top to the National Trust. It's in almost exactly the same state as she left it, full of her furniture and old photographs. Victorians always look so glum in photos. They stare solemnly back at the camera, with puritan seriousness. Not Beatrix though. She grinned naughtily in every picture. Like she'd just stolen some apples and hidden them in her bra. I liked her immediately.

The cosy house was crammed full of National Trust volunteers in the same geek's livery of wool and glasses. They were straining at the bit to regale visitors with Beatrix Potter facts. Each volunteer ruthlessly competitive, interrupting one another and pedantically correcting any slightly errant trivia. There were two particularly militant helpers, a pair of elderly ladies who occupied the study, where presumably Beatrix penned *The Filthy Billionaire*. '*The Tale of Peter Rabbit* was published in October 1903,' said the first woman. 'Well actually, Beatrix originally self-published the book in 1900,' replied the second, smugly. 'Yes well, it was *properly* published in October 1903,' shot back the tetchy first lady. 'Ummm, I think you mean it was properly published in October *1902*,' grinned the second. 'Oh just … shit off, Betty!' snapped the first, to the obvious shock of the throngs of gathered children and their furious parents. I laughed like a drain.

It was time for lunch and I found a pub in John Ruskin's home village of Coniston. I sat alone by the log fire devouring a pie and a tankard of ale, like a medieval knight. I was the only person in the pub. Finally another couple came in. They looked trendy and urban. I had nothing to do but people-watch and eavesdrop, so this was great news. The couple inspected the menu on the blackboard above the bar. 'What's the vegetarian option, please?' said the lady to the barwoman. 'Salmon,' she replied bluntly, with a Lancastrian warble. 'Ummm … sorry, I'm a vegetarian, I don't eat fish,' said the lady as diplomatically as possible. 'What sort of vegetarian doesn't eat fish!' exclaimed the barwoman. 'Jesus Christ. There's that many vegetarians I can't keep up! I like eating meat and that's that.' This was baffling logic by anyone's standards. 'OK. No worries … no biggie. Is there a salad I could have perhaps?' she said. 'We've got chicken nuggets?' said the barwoman. 'I'll just have a white wine spritzer, please,' said the woman, who, as a vegetarian, probably didn't have the strength to carry on the fight. 'Coming right up,' said the barwoman, 'And just to let you know pork scratching, are half price at the moment.' The couple sat down next to each other and snogged like teenagers. I resented them for their happiness.

That afternoon I headed to Dove Cottage. I took the guided tour and was told all about Wordsworth's life, work, and the fact that in seven years as Poet Laureate he failed to write a single poem. It was a fascinating insight into his creative process. But with my brain addled by sadness, all I could think was, I wonder if the Poet Laureate qualifies for a Nando's black card? I had one last destination on my literary tour, visiting Greta Hall, the former home of Wordsworth's great friend, fellow poet and opium addict Samuel Coleridge. That was the plan anyway, but as I drew into Keswick I saw a sign daubed with the image of an enormous pencil and I got distracted. I pulled into the car park and found a yellow billboard informing me that I'd arrived at the 'world's only pencil museum'. They say imitation is the sincerest form of flattery, well, the fact that no one on Planet Earth has thought to copy this breathtaking format perhaps says everything that needs to be said about the pencil museum.

The entry fee was five pounds, which seemed steep. But then again the museum did contain the world's biggest pencil. On the way in you walk through a faux graphite mine and beyond lie some of the most boring exhibits ever conceived. Slapped in enormous font on the wall was this brilliant gag: 'Did you hear the joke about the pencils? Never mind, it's pointless.' Hilarious, right? Apart from the fact that it doesn't actually make any sense. Because a pencil isn't point-less. It has a point at the end of it, the nib. A pencil without a point is not a pencil, is it? It's a stick. They were clearly struggling to fill the museum. For some reason, mounted on a wall, there's a picture of radio DJ Chris Evans's face made entirely out of pencils. The relevance is not revealed. There are also lots of photos of the Queen and the Duke of Edinburgh opening Cumberland Pencil Factory, with poor old Liz wandering about trying to look like she gives the tiniest toss about pencils. I don't know how the Queen does it. She must wake up every day and ask, 'What bollocks am I up to today?' and get told, 'Oh, you're driving to Yeovil to celebrate the fiftieth anniversary of the opening of the national ironing board museum.' Then I imagine she just slaps a palm into her forehead, and says 'Screw this: I'm going for a dump,' before disappearing into the bog with a copy of the *Express*.

I felt embarrassed queuing up for a ticket. This was a museum for children and families. It was not for single, adult men. And I looked sheepishly at my feet as I uttered the depressing sentence, 'Ticket for one please'. So I felt like a bit of a loser before I had even entered the graphite mine. But the apex of my loneliness was taking a selfie with the world's longest pencil. This was the bleakest moment of my journey so far. What had happened to my life? What was I doing here, miles away from home, alone, in a fucking pencil museum? I texted Dave the photo. He messaged back almost immediately. 'Glad you've seen the world's biggest pencil. I've got the world's biggest rubber in my bedroom.' I was glad he could see the funny side. And he did indeed have a box of extra-large condoms in his bedside table. He bought them in the pharmacy in Austin in the ludicrous hope that he might 'grow into them'. I pined for that time again. That trip to America felt exciting. But I'd lost my way since then. It didn't feel like I was winning at life anymore. It felt the opposite. I felt pathetic. Yes, I was in one of the most imposing and magnificent landscapes in the world but the beauty felt empty without someone to share it with. It felt wasted on me. I was sick of wandering as lonely as a cloud. Wordsworth wrote that '*Through love, through hope, and faith's transcendent dower, we feel that we are greater than we know.*' But driving back home from the Lake District

I felt loveless, hopeless and I was beginning to lose all faith in My Groupon Adventure.

Chapter Fifteen

The news about Jen had detonated bomb-like beneath me, and I was still staggering around shell-shocked and bloodied in the ruins. I'd been humiliated and the finality of seeing the woman I loved with somebody else had left me bereft. I was a mosaic man. I looked exactly the same but shattered into a thousand pieces. So I did the only thing I could possibly do to forget about the pain. I did lots and lots of Groupons. Groupon had started as a pole with which to vault myself into a better life, now it had become a crutch. But I couldn't see another solution. The superficial distraction of novelty was the only thing that could drown out the trumpets of catastrophe that rang oppressively in my mind. First up, I spent fifty quid on a 'Sports Mascot Experience'. And so I ended up moonlighting as the mascot for Bristol Rugby Club. For one day only I was 'Brizzley Bear'.

I was told to get changed in the cleaning cupboard opposite the home dressing room. Which meant that in the eyes of Bristol Rugby Club I was about as important as Cif. I left the door open in case I passed out from the bleach fumes. The rugby lads had also left their changing room door wide open, and so I could see straight in. Twenty-two granite giants strapped up their meaty hamstrings, tied their boots and punched their own shoulders in preparation for the ensuing physical confrontation. These hulking monsters looked at me with abject pity. We were all adult men, but they were about to go to war in a heroic battle of brawn and brain, and I was about to pretend to be a bear for 80 minutes. I felt tragic.

I suppose I shouldn't have expected any respect from adults. Mascots are for kids really. And the children love Brizzley in Bristol. They swarm you as you walk around the pitch like wasps. So my main job was giving all of them high fives and fist bumps. The younger ones find it magical, the older ones just try and rip your head off. One particular spotty teenager tried to set my ears on fire. The suit is heavy, ungainly and boiling hot.

But the worst part is the smell. It's hard to put into words the odour haunting that costume. But if you imagine taking the scrotums of a thousand tramps, dehydrating them in the hot sun, and then crumbing them up into potpourri – you'll get pretty close.

The guy who normally dons the suit is a bloke called Dan. He showed me the ropes before the match, teaching me the classic moves like the wave, the high five, and the sassy finger wag. Then Dan told me that his signature move as Brizzley Bear was 'the worm'. THE WORM! So every time I walked around the pitch, I was met with a relentless chorus of drunken Bristolian oiks screaming 'DO THE WORM! DO THE WORM BRIZZLEY! BRIZZLEY BEAR! DO THE WORM!' Now, quick newsflash guys: I can't do the worm. That might shock you, I know. But I can't be cool in *every way*. But I'm not a stick in the mud: I attempted to pacify the braying crowd with a hastily improvised robot. And I tried to twerk, but they weren't interested. All they wanted was the worm. And so for the whole match they chanted: 'DO THE WORM BRIZZLEY!'

The clock clicked to 78 minutes. I was now only two minutes away from the end of my shift. I'd so far managed to avoid doing the worm. But all of a sudden, stood by the family stand, a steward tries to steamroller me into doing it. 'WHO WANTS TO SEE BRIZZLEY DO THE WORM?' he roared. The crowd erupt. I was furious and thinking, I'm going to maul this prick. I'm going to rip his face off. And then I remembered I wasn't actually a real bear. I tried to whisper to the steward that I couldn't actually do the worm, but this is incredibly difficult to do if you have a furry spaceship for a head. He couldn't hear me above the relentless chorus of 'WORM! WORM! WORM!'

and the slow handclaps. All of a sudden it dawned on me: I'm actually going to have to do the worm in front of fifteen thousand people! How had it come to this? If this is what being spontaneous gets you, then I didn't want to be spontaneous anymore.

So I went for it. And it wasn't a great worm. People booed. A five-year-old girl threw her burger at me. A man in a wheelchair ripped up his season ticket. A pensioner did a dirty protest into her hat. I'd let the fans down, I'd let Bristol Rugby Club down, I'd let Dan down. I'd brought shame on the Brizzley brand. But at least the ordeal was over. I got changed in the cleaning cupboard and drove home. CUT TO: the Monday morning after. Dan checks the Brizzley Bear Twitter account, (which exists!), and this is what he finds:

WHAT! I was now being trolled by a 12-year-old boy because I can't do the worm. How had this happened to my life? This wasn't the plan at all. When I accidentally stumbled across Groupon all those months ago, I might just have had a curious browse and then moved onto the next internet novelty, perhaps a blog featuring photos of dogs in bikinis, or a video of a cat that can bake. But I didn't. I sprinted into the smoke because I felt exhilarated by the buffet of possibility that lay in front of me. But now I realised I had lost control. Groupon had taken over my life. It was no longer excitement and possibility driving me forwards, but desperation. I was addicted.

They say the opposite of addiction is not sobriety, but connection. We turn to toxic distractions because we are lonely, so the argument goes. And I was lonely. I'd barely seen Dave since I got back from America, I was harrowingly single, and I'd been ignoring my other friends as I poured all my time and focus into this Sisyphean pursuit of novelty. All my priorities had become warped. Rather than a means to a noble end, Groupon had become an end in itself. I had this feeling that with these constant new adventures I was running away from something. But I couldn't put my finger on exactly what. Slowly Groupon was crowding everything else out of my life.

Things came to a head one Saturday in mid-July. Dave had somehow managed to join a Fleetwood Mac tribute band called Fleetwood Snack. This was the secret project he'd been keeping hushed up. And they were playing the biggest gig of their careers on the John Orange Peel Stage at the Glastonbudget festival in Leicester. It was a big deal. And Dave had rung me to ask me to come and support. 'This is our big shot,' he said, 'it will be swarming with industry bigwigs. If we nail this then next year we could be invited to "The European Battle of the Tribute Bands" in Dusseldorf.' This was his Everest. Fleetwood Snack weren't quite headlining. That honour had gone to Abbatoir, an Abba tribute band made up of four farmers from Somerset. The Meatloaf tribute act Canned Meat would be a contender too. 'This such a great opportunity for us,' he said. 'Yes, we're only on the John Orange Peel stage this year, but next year we might be asked to play the Toblerone stage. Plus there will be tons of agents watching. Anyone who is anyone in the wedding entertainment scene will be there. Cold Plaice had a great gig last year and now they've gone part-time at the fishmongers.'

'I can't make it, Dave, I'm really sorry.' I said down the phone. Dave was silent, so I ploughed on. 'I'm doing a Groupon … I'm spending the day at an owl sanctuary near Reading.' 'You're missing the biggest day of my life to go to a fucking owl sanctuary?' he said. 'Have you lost your mind?' Dave was very angry. I hadn't heard him this upset since H from Steps was evicted from *Celebrity Big Brother 7*. 'This beggars belief, that you'd miss the most important gig of my life to go to an owl sanctuary!' 'But they have the widest selection of tawny owls in the south Berkshire area?' I said. 'And their paninis are some of the best in Greater Basingstoke.' Dave hung up.

The next day I drove down to Feathers and Fur Falconry Centre in Twyford. And as Dave prepared to take the stage at Glastonbudget, I spent the afternoon hanging out with various birds of prey. The centre was run by a lady called Sadie, who's dedicated her entire life to falconry. This is how much Sadie loves falconry: one day every year she has to put on a special hat, go and stand in a field, and wait while a series of falcons have sex with her head so Sadie can collect their semen for breeding. It's falcon *bukkake*, basically. So next time you're having a bad day at work, ask yourself 'Do I have 15 falcons ejaculating on to my head?' Realise that you don't and count your blessings. In fact, why not get that phrase made into a motivational fridge magnet and stick it up in the office kitchen? That way all your colleagues can enjoy that bullet of pithy wisdom. It would be great for morale. It could even become a company motto. ('Darren, I know your wife's pregnant, but I'm afraid we're going to have to let you go. But as we say, at least you don't have 15 falcons jizzing on your head.')

First up at the centre, Sadie showed off her barn owls. Barn owls aren't that fancy. They are entry level owls. Even so, it was hard to enjoy their simple beauty as I was already getting texts from Dave. 'I hope you're enjoying the owls JUDAS!' sniped the first. Sadie showcased the tawny owls next and, as she was about to land one on my outstretched arm, my pocket vibrated with another message from Dave. 'A Henry VIII lookalike has just picked up a corporate gig in Monaco. Fingers crossed. PS. YOU'RE A JUDAS.' By the time I'd typed and sent an apologetic reply Sadie had unveiled an Indian owl too, which was the size of a large toddler. The tawny owl didn't seem to like the Indian owl, repeatedly squawking at it in a way that suggested he was saying: 'Bloody Indian owls, coming over here, eating our mice.' It was then finally time for Sadie to unleash the falcons, who seemed very excited to see her. We fed them a few dead chicks and then Sadie drew the session to a close. As I walked back to the car-park my phone buzzed with yet another text. 'Just got off stage. Absolutely killed it. We played "Little Lies" and IT WENT OFF. But you missed it didn't you? You massive bellend.'

An hour later I was sat in a local pub, alone with my thoughts. As I sat sipping my drink I thought back to Kendal and my collision with Gary the lonely psychopath. Was I turning into him? Perhaps that evening in the pub was a glimpse of my Christmas future? I shivered at the prospect. The owl sanctuary had been interesting enough. But I found it hard to enjoy the experience when I knew how much I'd betrayed my best friend. Dave had helped me discover Groupon in the first place, and he'd done so much to help me on my journey, yet I'd just thrown it straight back in his face. I'd been selfish and mean. But what was most worrying was that I'd known all this at the time and yet I still made the decision to choose the Groupon over him. It had nothing to do with Jen or winning the bet anymore. Adventure was all I had left and I was finding it impossible to wean myself off it, no matter how important the alternative was. Dave stopped returning my calls. I'd lost the love of my life and now I'd lost my best friend too. He was tired of waiting for me while I whittled away my days worshipping at the temple of spontaneity. My Groupon obsession had driven him away. Things were bad. But I still hadn't seen the worst of it.

Chapter Sixteen

I was becoming disillusioned with Groupon. Spontaneity hadn't turned out to be the elixir it had promised to be. Yet I was still ploughing money I didn't have into the Groupon fruit machine. The unhappier I got, the more I needed new adventures to help me escape myself. And the following morning I received an e-mail from Groupon offering me the chance to buy a DNA test. Immediately I was intrigued by the Pandora's Box that lurked within my chromosomes. Because, what makes us who we are? Is it nature or nurture? Many people answer these questions about identity by resorting to genetics: we are our DNA, they say. But do we really know our own DNA? People often say things like 'It's in my genes', without any evidence whatsoever. They just see a part of their personality, perhaps a strength or a flaw, and automatically trace it back to their genetic heritage. 'I'm fat because of my genes. My mum's fat, my dad's fat, my nan's fat – I was always going to be fat: it's in my DNA.' Could be. Or it could be all that cake DNA you stuff down your throat.

For most of human history we had no way of knowing of our genetic map. DNA tests have been a luxury reserved for the cast of freaks wheeled out on the Jeremy Kyle show. But now they'd become easily commercially available and so I decided to take one. The process was simple. The company couriered me a plastic vial and all I had to do was spit in it and send it back.

They'd then analyse my saliva in the lab and let me know the secrets of my genes. A couple of days later I received my results. I learned that, not only was I carrying the gene for ginger hair, but also the story of both my father- and mother-line ancestry.

On my father's side, it turns out that my heritage is Scandinavian. My Y-chromosome marker is I-S142, which is very, very rare in the UK. That makes me pretty special on these shores. I'm a strutting genetic anomaly. I'm literally a different breed. My Scandinavian roots also explain my previously unfathomable lust for grey polar necks, hot glögg, and pickled herring. My mother-line DNA marker is 'H1', which originated in West Asia 25,000 years ago, and then slowly migrated across Europe. West Asia comprises the Middle East, which helps explain my apathy towards democracy and disdain for the decadent West. I also share 50% of my DNA with a banana. Which explains a weird fantasy I have of being chopped up and then covered in toffee and whipped cream.

Having a DNA test did highlight the absurdity of racism. Whenever anyone tells you that they are '100% British and proud' remind them that one in 200 men are directly descended from the murderous Mongolian warlord Genghis Khan. But all in all, the £250 I'd spent on my DNA test was a total waste of money. I now knew where my ancestors came from. The harder question to answer was 'so what?' It didn't stop me spending money, though. Hours after my results I noticed Groupon had emailed me this offer:

And I bought it immediately. WHAT WAS WRONG WITH ME? In my unstable mental state, it seemed a perfectly sensible thing to do. I was a new person now, I reasoned, so I of course I needed a new name. Plus I'd become deeply unhappy, but a new name would represent a fresh start. And after all, the UK Deed Poll website had a number of testimonials from happy customers. Including this one:

> 'I rang the Deed Poll and the young lady was very helpful. Made my payment over the phone. Received in a couple of days.'
> **Peter Cockburn**, Berkshire. September 2013.

Being called Mr Cockburn is a tough cross to bear. If I'd struggled on internet dating as a fully fledged lord, Old Cockburn was probably having a nightmare. There was a silver lining I suppose: at least his first name wasn't 'Savage'. On the face of it my name doesn't look too bad in comparison. My name is 'Max Dickins', or to give you my full name 'Max Harry Sebastian Wilfred Ewan Dickins'. I was named after my father. And Mum says it could have been any of those guys. But everyone seems to struggle with 'Max Dickins'. People always spell it Max Dick*ens*, and then ask me whether I'm related to the writer Charles Dickens. I've actually stopped correcting people who spell it wrong, I haven't got the energy. Not unless it's absurdly incorrect. British Gas once made out a bill to 'Axe Dickend', which is less a name, and more a request. So, I had often thought of changing my name for sheer convenience, but also because 'Max Dickins' just isn't very showbiz. It's hard to see it up in lights. Elton John did the same thing. He was christened as Reginald Dwight, but understandably changed it. Nobody is going to pay money to see someone called Reginald in concert.

So I decided it was finally time to bite the bullet and change my name. But I needed some inspiration. So that evening I posted this message on my Facebook account:

> 'I'm changing my name by Deed Poll to whatever your best suggestion is. Go nuts.'

And there were hundreds and hundreds of responses. The first to come in was:

Ulrich Van Der Hoogstraaten

I loved it! So much of the motivation behind getting a new name was throwing off my old identity. My Groupon Adventure had changed me. I was living a different life now, full of risk and fun and spontaneity. Groupon was the tool I'd used to create a new me, and I needed a new name to match. Max Dickins sounds like a data inputter from Slough who still lives with his mum. Ulrich Van Der Hoogstraaten sounds like a dildo entrepreneur with a pet cheetah.

More and more suggestions flooded in:

Troy Spectacular	Pardon Me
Noah Swallows	Cornfed Hen
Lance Turtleneck	The Hotel Brothers
The Plan	Turgid Steel
Ghost Cop	Notta Spy
Fax Me	Moist Cake
Mr Prick Whimper	Twelve Inches
Shandy Mattress	The Woolf
Weepy Rugs	Wasabi Burns
Dirty Naan	Whattha Dickens

Publicity Stunt	The Feast
Lone Gunman	Minty Clam
Blonathan Dunce	Rempklt Sassoon

There are clearly some great names there, and weirdly I regularly get spam e-mails from a lot of them already. But there are some rules when you change your name by Deed Poll. For example, it can't be offensive, so I was forced to immediately rule these suggestions out:

Black Guy	Cleaveland Steamer
Peter The Rapist	Roger Mee
Christ	Dick Blisters
Captain Fanny Smasher	Clive Bastard
Crumbly Gash	Mucky Dickend

And according to Deed Poll guidelines the names must also be pronounceable. So these were out too:

Malcolm Muhlnumnuhmehrr
やなはワム

It also must not contain numbers, symbols or punctuation marks. So these too were gone:

Dirk Sad?	Oleg's Bollock-Hammock
Mine's The Beef	I'm Spartacus
That's Not My Hat	

But there can be no copyright protection of names, your name is a free-for-all brandwise. So these were all fine:

Justin Bieber	Ask Jeeves
Sir Trevor McDonald	Batman
Lil Wayne	Whoopi Goldberg
Google It	Tim Henman

So what did I go for? I was keen on Ulrich Van Der Hoogstraaten, but if I got irritated by people misspelling Dickins, then that would be like leaping straight from the frying pan into not just a fire, but a nuclear reactor of clerical errors. Also, I decided that I wanted to keep my first name. Otherwise the confusion would be terrible. If I changed my name to 'The Woolf', say, then someone trying to get my attention would just end up shouting 'The, The, The, The, The,' repeatedly, and I'd obviously ignore them, assuming they had a stutter. So my new name would be Max *Something*. But what was that 'Something'? I thought, 'Surely it has to be a nod to my new dogma? Surely it has to be a manifestation of my new ideology? Surely my new name has to be: *Max Groupon*? So in June 2014 I changed my name legally by Deed Poll to 'Max Groupon'. Here's my new passport:

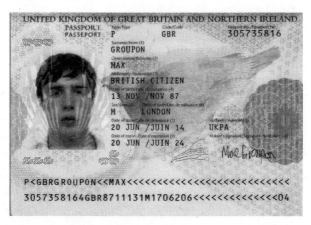

I don't recommend changing your name by Deed Poll. There's a lot of admin to take care of. For example, I had to call up Santander again:

I'd clearly properly lost my mind now, and things quickly began to get very dark very quickly. I suddenly went through a weird phase of buying products from Groupon and customising them with pictures of my own face. For example, I bought myself a personalized birthday cake:

It wasn't even my birthday. But it was just nice to have a cake that I didn't have to defrost. I'd like to pretend that the cake was an isolated incident of egotism, but I'd be lying. In late July I spent an entire Sunday building a 150-piece puzzle of my own face:

In hindsight, it's very hard to explain my behaviour. Why exactly was I doing all this? I think buying stuff with my face on it felt like an affirmation of my self-worth, a way of rebuilding the ego that had been so wounded by the romantic rejection I'd just relived a couple of weeks previously. My warped mind continued to convince me to splurge. There were playing cards; there were scatter cushions; there was a teddy bear; there was an enormous wall mural. All with my face on. But it got worse. I also bought this:

It's a double duvet with my face on it. It cost £150. That's not an affirmation of self-worth: that's a cry for help. And it looks like I've got mumps. You're probably wondering why I'm showing you this atrocity; after all, let's face it, it is horrendously embarrassing. The truth is that I'm showing you the duvet because by putting it in a book, a double duvet with my face on it actually becomes tax deductible. I genuinely slept under that duvet for a while, which led to one very awkward confrontation with a builder. It's a short story but an embarrassing one: one day I realised that I needed some shelves. So, I rang up a furniture shop to place an order. The bloke on the phone said, 'No problem, Lord Groupon, they should be with you tomorrow anytime between 9 and 5'. 'Can you not be more specific mate?' I said. 'No sir, anytime between 9 and 5,' he replied.

Anyway, the delivery guy eventually turned up with my shelves and the deal was that he would build them for me. So the builder brings the flat-pack into my bedroom and sees the duvet. He's totally lost for words, staring at it, jaw ajar. He finally spoke. 'Have I had a stroke? Or is that your face?' I confirm that: yes, the photo on my duvet is indeed my face. 'That's the weirdest thing I've ever seen,' he said. 'And what the hell are those?' 'Oh, they're vibrating buttock pads,' I said. 'You're odd, mate.' I tried to win him round by offering to make him a cup of tea. 'Oh yeah, I'd love a cup of tea, thanks,' he said. 'Sure,' I said, 'I'll go and make you one. Should be with you anytime between now and five o'clock tomorrow.' He refused to build the shelves. He just sat on the end of my bed and crossed his arms until I brought him a tea, which I served in a mug with my face on. It was at this point that he walked out.

I'd had enough now. I was completely demoralised. I'd lost everything: the love of my life, my best friend, and even my name. And now (finally) I'd lost my faith in spontaneity too. My new lifestyle suddenly felt totally vacuous, and I saw Groupon as the false idol it was. Back at the beginning of my journey I thought that filling up my life with new experiences, with new things, would make it feel less empty. I had poured Groupons into my life as if were a bucket, believing that once it was full I'd be happy again. But now I'd realised that life isn't like a bucket at all. It's got a massive hole in the bottom. It's more of a tube. You can never fill the bucket up – it's futile.

That evening I promised myself that I wouldn't do any more Groupons. This was it. Game over. I didn't care about the bet anymore. I would throw the towel in and take the Groupon from Hell on the chin. I still had a bunch of vouchers outstanding, but I wouldn't fulfil them. I texted Dave to see if he fancied using them instead. It was my way of saying sorry. I really missed him. But he didn't reply. And I began a rapid descent back to square one. The girls had gone off on holiday together, so I spent a fortnight alone on the sofa in my pants with just the TV for company. I watched *Bargain Hunt* religiously every lunchtime; I entered online spelling bee competitions in which I lost to six-year-olds from South Korea; I rang up *Babestation* just for a chat. I was behaving as if the previous 8 months hadn't happened at all. My life became unilaterally grey again. Plus, I was staring down the barrel of yet another humiliation. Because I still didn't have a date for my cousin's wedding which was now looming at the end of August.

Then one evening, I'd just sat down with a family-sized lasagne ready to watch an entire series of *Master Chef Australia*, when the doorbell rang. It was Dave. He had a six-pack of lager and eyes full of forgiveness. 'I think we need to talk,' he said. He came in and surveyed the scene. 'Is everything alright, mate?' he said. 'Yeah. Why?' I asked. He pointed at the sofa where I had been resting my head on a pillow with my face it on it, snuggling under a duvet with my face on it, whilst drinking out of a mug with my face on it. 'Groupon,' I said. 'Right,' said Dave, handing me a can. 'Christ, you've got a lot of candles.' I went into the kitchen and retrieved a second spoon so Dave and I could finish my ready meal together. It was like that scene from *Lady and the Tramp*, but instead of spaghetti it was lasagne, and instead of the Lady there was just another tramp.

It was time to clear the air. 'I'm sorry, Dave,' I said. 'I lost the plot there for a bit with this Groupon bullshit. But don't worry. I've chucked it all in now. I want things to go back to how they were.' 'Are you kidding?' said Dave. 'Why would you want things to go back to how they were? When you were boring, and heartbroken, and unhappy, and overweight?' This was the first time Dave had mentioned I'd been overweight. 'Look where that lifestyle's got me,' I said, holding up a teddy bear with my face on it for emphasis. 'Yes, OK, you've made some mistakes, but you've also had some amazing experiences too.' He had a point. The path of adventure had shown me a brilliant time. But I was confused. 'Dave, don't you want to win the bet?' 'I've already won the bet! You've missed two weeks! I will make you do your punishment – don't worry about that. But there are more important things at stake.' 'You've changed,' I said.

'Do you know what?' continued Dave. 'I've never told you this because ... well, just because, but your Groupon thing made me really proud of you. And more than that, it really inspired me to take on my own adventure. It made me join that band, do you know that? I've always wanted to do it, but I've always been too scared. But after we wrestled those alligators, I just thought, fuck it. You know? Like, what's the worst that could happen?' I was about to say that being in a Fleetwood Mac tribute band was probably the actual worst-case scenario, but it felt churlish so I just nodded. 'And, yes you missed our really important gig, and yes, I thought you were a massive prick, but do you know what? At least you missed it because you were doing something *interesting*. Last year you would have missed it because you had a tricky transfer window to negotiate on Football Manager.'

Dave was right. It was a tricky transfer window. I'd just got Norwich promoted to the Premier League and the big boys were now sniffing around my best players. But Dave was also right in another respect. I had changed as a person. I was more adventurous. I was more open-minded. I was now excited by uncertainty: optimistically seeing possibility rather than fearfully finding threat. But the difference was that now I no longer saw the value in adventure at all. It felt superficial and shallow. It had none of the rich subtleties you get from immersion in a special person or a treasured hobby. It was like I was always grazing on sweets, rather than sitting down and enjoying a long, nutritious meal. And what's more, I'd realised that adventure was only enjoyable insofar as I could share that experience with somebody else. But Groupon had alienated me from everyone I loved.

I explained all this to Dave. 'What I want Dave, I suppose, more than anything else, is something to pour myself into,' I said. 'What, like, a cup? You want a cup?' 'No, not literally, Dave. Metaphorically. And maybe not something, but *someone*.' 'So you want a bird?' he said. 'Yes, I suppose,' I said. Because maybe love is what I needed? Because after all, love isn't just another experience that slips through the sieve of consciousness. It's a state of grace. It's a way of transcending the bucket. 'And do you think you're likely to meet someone sat on the sofa? Feeling sorry for yourself?' said Dave. 'I've got Skype?' I said. Dave rolled his eyes and put down his beer.

'Don't you see that Groupon was just a tool? It was a means to an end! Groupon was your coach. Max, this whole project, this whole Groupon thing you've been doing, hasn't been about Groupon at all. It's been about creating a mindset. It's been about cultivating a way of seeing the world. And you've done that. And now you're going to throw it all away, for what? Why? Because you got bored? Because you've made some bad decisions? Because some girl you've creepily pursued for 8 months has pied you off?' I'd never seen Dave so passionate. Not since the 10-minute argument he'd had with a hotelier in Devon about the illegitimacy of tomatoes in a fried breakfast. 'Groupon has given you this gift, Max, this superpower: the power to go out into the world and shake it. To shake the tree of life because you have a cast iron faith that if you shake it hard enough that the fruit will fall straight into your hands. And yes, you've used this superpower badly. You've mainly used it to customise various soft furnishings with photos of your face. But now is your chance to use it for good, not evil. Because isn't that all dating is? To go from tree to tree, shaking them until, despite the impossible odds, you find someone wonderful?' 'Well, if you put it like that,' I said. 'So for God's sake, stop feeling sorry for yourself and put yourself out there.'

I spontaneously gave Dave a hug, which surprised us both. 'Thanks, mate,' I said. 'I needed that.' 'No worries,' said Dave, 'Just remember: imagination is the key. 'Cos you're your own destiny. You never should be lonely. When time is on your side.' 'That's another S Club 7 lyric isn't it, Dave?' 'Yup. From "Bring it All Back". But those words could have come from any prophet. Jesus, Buddha, Rick Astley. Anyone. Wise words mate, wise words.' We hugged again. 'Dave, my cousin wants your band to play at his wedding if you're up for it?' I said. 'He'll pay you?' Dave looked like he was about to cry. 'Are you sure, mate?' 'Absolutely certain mate. His fiancée loves Fleetwood Mac.' 'Oh mate! We won't let him down! We need a break. The wedding circuit is tough to break into. Fleetwood Crack has got it sewn up. But they've got a big label behind them so ...' 'What, like Universal Records or something?' I said. 'No. They're with Fat Barry's Variety Smorgasbord.' 'Right.' 'He's a heavy hitter. And not just because he's fat.' 'You'll be great,' I said. Dave got up to go to the toilet.

Dave had helped me see the light. I did need to put myself out there. But how? Internet dating was an option, but that had proved very hit-and-miss. Another option was to go from bar to bar asking girls out, but I didn't have time for that. I needed something much more efficient. I barely had 21 days till the wedding. So realistically I needed to meet someone significant as soon as possible. No, I had to find a totally new strategy. I needed to think outside of the box. Pursuing girls had not worked. But perhaps there was a way to do the absolute opposite? Perhaps there was a way I could get people to come *to me*? To beat a path to my door. I took a spoonful of lasagne into my mouth and gazed thoughtfully out the window. Suddenly my phone buzzed on the coffee table in front of me. I picked it up and inspected the screen. Yet another e-mail from Groupon. Like a seething Hydra, every time I sliced one head off it was replaced by two more. I'd done over 100 deals but I could not slay this monster. Then it hit me. Was there a way for people to buy me in the same way that I'd bought all these Groupon offers? Of course there was! The solution had been staring me right in the face: I was going to try and sell myself on Groupon. To defeat Groupon I would have to *become Groupon*.

Yes, it was the one thing I swore I would never do. The thing I'd chastised the stripogram for in America. Sure, I had previously said that selling yourself on Groupon was seedy and undignified and desperate. But this would solve all my problems in one fell swoop and I am nothing if not a hypocrite. This bonkers idea would be my biggest adventure yet. Me back at my spontaneous best: the alligator wrestling me, not the corrupted version I'd become. If things worked out, Groupon and I were going to have one last hurrah. 'What the hell is this?' said Dave, stood in the living room doorway with his pants around his ankles. He was holding a roll of toilet paper with my face on it. I smiled back: 'Dave, I've got a plan ...'

Chapter Seventeen

'When I said, "put yourself out there", I didn't mean this,' said Dave as we bounced off the Tube at London Bridge. I didn't want to be doing this either. But Groupon hadn't played ball. I'd spent the past week sending them hundreds of e-mails and they hadn't replied to one of them. Not even to tell me to bugger off. They'd simply ignored me. All I wanted was a small favour. And after all, they owed me one. I'd spent thousands upon thousands of pounds buying from their website. And now I wanted to become a Groupon deal myself. So I'd politely asked Groupon to sell 'a date with me' on their website. And they had rudely looked in the opposite direction. Which is how Dave and I ended up here: walking over London Bridge, holding a big placard with 'Help me Groupon' scrawled across it in blue marker pen. I wasn't going to leave until I got the answer I wanted. Because with the wedding looming, I was in a rush.

I positioned myself on the pavement in front of their four-storey office, near Bank. And I began to chant. '*What do I want? A DATE! When do I want it? SOON-ISH! In the next week or so is fine. A fortnight tops.*' It wasn't the catchiest protest slogan ever conceived, but it contained all the key information. I felt energised. I'd been to the Mountain Top and seen the Promised Land. So I stood with my sign held defiantly aloft above my head, bellowing my message at the ambivalent glass façade,

believing it was surely only a matter of time before I was allowed in. Soon Groupon employees gathered at the windows to stare and point. Nervous security guards eyeballed me. Dave sat on a bollard nearby looking embarrassed. But he only had himself to blame. It was his intervention that had led us here.

Breakthroughs in important causes take time. It took the suffragettes over 20 years to win women the right to vote, for example. So I knew that if I were to score an equally brave victory, then I would need to be as resolute and patient. But after 20 minutes of protest I got bored, and made a bolt for the revolving door. On the other side lay a hip-high electronic gate. I momentarily considered vaulting it and rushing into the lift. But before I could make my move, I got fingered by the receptionist (metaphorically). 'Excuse me, sir, do you have an appointment?' she said. 'Errr … yes?' I replied, unconvincingly. 'With whom?' she said. 'Umm … with Groupon.' 'Right. And with whom specifically, within Groupon?' 'Errr … Steve?' I said. 'Steve?' 'Yes, Steve.' 'Steve who?' 'You know! Big Steve!' I said. 'I'm not aware of a Big Steve. What's his surname?' 'Umm …

Smith?' I gambled. 'There is nobody at Groupon with that name, sir.' 'Right. What about Steve Potter?' 'There is nobody called Steve Potter, either sir.' 'Steve Warner?' 'Sir, are you just guessing various surnames?' 'No. Steve Spielberg?' 'I'm going to have to ask you to leave, sir. We can only let you in if you have an appointment.' Bloody jobsworth. Did she not know who I was? I was Lord Max Groupon. The man single-handedly keeping the Groupon share price afloat. She should have been piggybacking me up the stairs.

Storming the barricades hadn't worked. So I continued to wait hopefully on the street outside, singing my pithy jingle. Another two hours passed without success. It was time for Plan C. I took to barracking people on their way into the office, begging them to tell someone important that Lord Max Groupon was stood inches away from the Pearly Gates. This was not a popular tactic. And soon an irate South African security guard informed Dave and I that, if we didn't leave, he was going to call the police. 'Don't worry, Dave, we're not doing anything illegal,' I said, full of bravado. 'What's your problem, mate?' I said, 'I'm not hurting anyone, am I?' 'You might be a terrorist,' he said in an unintelligible Afrikaans brogue. 'Pardon?' I was genuinely baffled by his pronunciation. 'I said, you might be a terrorist!' he repeated angrily. South Africans really can't say the word terrorist in their accent. It just sounds like they're doing an impression of a machine gun. 'What sort of terrorist e-mails ahead?' I said. 'And what sort of terrorist turns up begging for a date? Say what you like about Osama bin Laden, but I don't think he was in it for the pussy.' The security guard called the police.

I was up against it now. I needed a result quickly before the fuzz turned up. Plus it was getting late. Dave had already bottled it and thrown in the towel, and I was about to head home too. Then suddenly a young woman emerged from the revolving door. 'Are you Max?' she said. 'Yes. Are you Groupon?' I said. 'Well, my name's Millie, but I work for Groupon.' 'Great! Did you get my e-mails?' 'Yes. You sent a lot didn't you?' 'Yes sorry about that. I'm getting a bit desperate.' 'Do you want to come up?' 'Errr! Yeah!' I said, my grin tumescent with gratitude. The security guard glared at me as I was led into the lift. Upstairs in the capacious office, battalions of scruffy techies pecked at their keyboards preparing the latest offers. Millie led me into a luminous green meeting room. 'Everyone's very excited because we've just launched a great deal on vibrators,' she said. It was like seeing behind the magician's curtain. Millie and I sat down opposite each other, and we were soon joined by Simon, the Groupon Head of Communications, and his assistant.

They all listened intently as I explained my situation and repeated my plea. When I'd finished speaking, Simon looked thoughtfully upwards and to the right. He was either thinking or trying to fart quietly. His assistant waited dutifully. Millie smiled back at me sympathetically. We were all hanging on his verdict. 'Alright,' he said, 'We'll do it. Why not? Sounds fun.' I punched the air. I'd done it! Victory was mine. Groupon had agreed to sell a date with me on their website. I was on the cusp of my biggest adventure yet. 'We won't be able to charge anything, obviously,' said Simon. 'Why not?' I said, a tad hurt. 'Well, otherwise you're a bit like a prostitute?' he said. 'I don't mind,' I shrugged. 'No, no. We'll make the voucher free. Run it like a competition,' he said. 'Could we not charge a little bit?' I said. 'I think people might be willing to pay a tenner to go on a date with me.' All three of them laughed in my face. This plan might have enhanced my dating prospects but it hadn't improved my self-esteem. Charging absolutely nothing technically made me worthless. But I wasn't really in a position to negotiate. All that mattered was that we had an agreement. And the rules of the deal were simple. I'd take one lucky winner out on an all-expenses date wherever they were in the country. And who knew where it might lead from there?

'We'll have to draw the winner at random,' said Simon. 'Competition rules and all that.' This new caveat had suddenly thrown a huge amount of risk into proceedings. I could be going on a date with literally anybody. It might be a transsexual Inuit from Alaska. I might have to go up to the Shetland Islands to have a shortbread and heroin supper with a trawler man. I might have to take a fundamentalist Christian out for a Burger King. My eyes glazed over as I imagined the horror of making small talk with a fully paid-up member of the God squad. 'Sex is the way into hell,' she'd say, 'And I'm here to save you … can I have an onion ring?' But I tried to stay positive. There was also an equally good chance I would meet someone amazing. And then it suddenly dawned on me that this had all been prophesied. I thought back to my session with the psychic, months previously. When Amber gave me a tarot card reading, she drew out The Fool:

This was the card that had resonated so strongly with me at the crux of my project. The Fool: an adventurer on a journey; leaping into the unknown, with a smile on his face and hope in his heart. But I hadn't understood the full picture of The Fool at the time. I realised now that I had missed a key detail. Look again at the card. So filled with excitement is the explorer that he might not look where he's going. He might fall off a cliff and come to great harm. But hang on! Who's that little critter with him? It's a small dog to warn the traveller of missteps. To remind him of what's really important. So it turns out that that Tarot card had told me what I needed all along! A dog! Well, not a dog as such. I wanted a girlfriend preferably. But the point was that an adventurer needs an accomplice. He needs a soulmate for the road. It seems that, in her own subtle way, Amber had warned me about the choppy waters I would soon sail into. And I was relieved to be finally heeding her advice. Better late than never. I told Simon I'd love to go ahead with the deal.

The date went live a couple of days after our meeting. Millie had since been in touch and asked me to send through a blurb for the deal. After a hundred drafts, I came up with this:

'Max Dickins (6ft 3) is a 26-year-old comedian who lives in Stockwell, South London with his two flatmates, Philippa and Hope. Last year, Max was dumped and lost his zest for life. Now slowly but surely he's got his passion back, one Groupon at a time. But now he wants someone to share the adventure with. Could that be you?'

I put a lot of thought into those words. It was nice to mention being dumped because it made me seem vulnerable, and ergo: sexier. And it's always good to mention that you live with girls, because people are much less likely to think that you're a sex criminal. But as if that seductive bumf was not enough, to help sell the sizzle even more, Groupon had also been in touch with Philippa and Hope to get some supporting testimonials. So these quotes also appeared on the deal:

'Max is a good guy on the whole, but he always lies about his height, so look out for that. He's 5'8" at most.'
Max's flatmate, Philippa

'If I was single, looking for laughter, and had lower standards, I'd definitely date him.'
Max's flatmate, Hope

But despite those backhanded compliments, the idea seemed to catch people's imaginations. Groupon launched the offer on a Tuesday morning and the following day I was front page news on the *Huffington Post*; I made headlines in the *Daily Star*; and I did an interview for a feature in *Real People* magazine. (If you've never heard of *Real People* magazine, then it's one of those magazines that have stories like 'I had a holiday romance … WITH A SQUID!') I was even featured in the prestigious

Western Daily Press, which, as you are probably aware, is Plymouth's number one newspaper. So word was getting out. Even Jen had heard about it. In fact, she sent me this text message:

> My Dad is registering on Groupon to try buy a date with you. I am sure this isn't what you had in mind.

That was literally the last thing I had in mind. We hadn't got on when Jen and I were dating. From memory, he would always introduce me to his friends as 'Jen's current boyfriend'. And so you can see that the chances of us hitting it off now, over a romantic candlelit dinner, were decidedly slim. He clearly thought that I was such a horrendous prospect that he should leap into the breach to protect other girls from being sucked into the same delusion. But apart from that nasty surprise, take-up for the deal was strong. Girls were getting in touch on Twitter letting me know that they'd made a purchase:

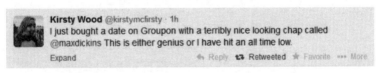

Kirsty Wood @kirstymcfirsty · 1h
I just bought a date on Groupon with a terribly nice looking chap called @maxdickins This is either genius or I have hit an all time low.
Expand   ← Reply ⇄ Retweeted ★ Favorite ••• More

I'm glad that a date with me constitutes an 'all time low'. But by the deadline a week later I'd sold almost a thousand dates. In fact, the offer had been so popular that Millie e-mailed to tell me, 'You're selling better than the dildos!' I now waited anxiously for Groupon to tell me the name of the lucky winner. There was a 1/1000 chance it could be my ex-girlfriend's dad. I was also genuinely worried that my mum might have secretly bought a date, as a sympathy purchase. After all, she had previous. When

I was growing up, there'd always be one Valentine's Day card waiting for me on the doormat. And I'd pick it up, giddy with excitement, and think, 'Oooh, who's this from? Maybe it's Hannah from the year above?' And then I'd open it and it would say '*Happy Valentine's Day darling! From your secret admirer, Mum*'. Which was both disappointing and creepy. But as if that threat wasn't enough, I was also terrified a man might buy the date. Nothing in the rules banned blokes. WHAT IF IT'S PSYCHOPATH SEB FROM TAXIDERMY? I thought, looking for a new body to stuff!

I was a menagerie of nerves. Every species of worry taking turns to howl into the black cavern of my mind. I listened to the whale CD for the first time in months to try to relax. And I stared at my phone, heart racing, eager to be put out of my misery. Hours went by without as much as a text. I became paranoid that my phone was broken. So I borrowed Philippa's mobile and rang my number. It went straight to voicemail. '*Hi this is David Hasselhoff. Max can't come to the phone right now, but if you leave your name and number after the beep, Max will call you back as soon as possible.*' I clearly had no signal. I cursed the terrible phone reception in our basement flat and decided to go for a walk. Suddenly my phone came to life. Six missed calls from Groupon. And one voice message. Groupon had been trying to get in touch all day and had been unable to get through. I rang them back straight away.

Simon told me that my date would be with someone called Alex Seabright. 'That's a very ambiguous name gender-wise,' I said. 'Are you sure it's a woman?' He said he had no idea. But there was nothing I could do. I would have to cross my fingers and hope for the best. So I e-mailed Alex to confirm a date and a time, and I booked a restaurant called Archipelago in Soho. They offered me the best table in the house, right by the window. Mainly I think because I booked it under the name Lord Groupon. The peerage had finally proved handy. That evening I told Phil and Hope the momentous news. 'Well, you better have another spray tan,' said Hope. 'And I can cut your hair!' said Phil. 'Absolutely no way,' I said. This time I wasn't going to take any chances. I wanted to do everything by myself.

The big day was soon upon me. I arrived slightly early and waited outside the restaurant. My stomach in knots every time someone walked past. Finally, I got a tap on the shoulder. I turned round and it was her. She was a woman and not my mother. I felt like weeping with relief. Simon from Groupon insisted on joining us for the date. He sat at a table on the other side of the restaurant throughout, trying not to look at us. Like a parent at a school disco. I think he came along to make sure I didn't attack her, which I found offensive. There are easier ways to murder someone than running a nationwide media campaign to find a victim – a point I made vociferously to Simon at the start of the date, inadvertently making him more determined to stay, on the basis that 'The Lady Doth Protest Too Much'. I didn't want him there. Dates are stressful enough as it is without having an audience.

After an hour of proceedings I'd come to the firm conclusion that Alex was mental. I couldn't get a word in edgeways. All she did was bang on about her ex. 'My ex had a personalized number plate. I mean, how self-obsessed can you get?' She said. And I was thinking, 'Jesus Christ, wait until you see my duvet.' After my second cocktail, I went to the toilet for a breather. I texted the girls: 'She's fully bonkers.' They replied instantly. 'You shouldn't be surprised. What sort of person buys a date on Groupon?' Fifteen minutes later I returned to the table. It had been so long that Alex probably now assumed I'd been for a dump, but I didn't really care at this stage. I needed that timeout. The menu at Archipelago is bizarre. To start with we had kangaroo skewers, zebra kebabs, and python carpaccio. Alex also ordered a side order of dried ants. There wasn't a triple-cooked chip in sight. The food seemed to relax her and we began to hit it off. We joshed about the starters, cooing at the weirdness. We coquettishly fed each other insects. I put two empty kebab skewers inside my top lip and pretended to be a walrus. She pretended to find that funny. It was world-class flirting. So good in fact, that I was actually now glad Simon was here to witness it. I could see him out of the corner of my eye shaking his head in what I assume was awestruck disbelief, in the same way you might at a heavenly Roger Federer backhand. Things were now going brilliantly well. Then for main course Alex ordered alpaca curry and I almost walked out.

It could have been something to do with the relentless torrent of exotic cocktails, but I was having a fantastic time now. My

voice was hoarse from laughing, and an enormous smile had gazumped all the nerves. Alex briefly excused herself to visit the ladies. And in these brief moments of solitude I had a chance to reflect on my evening so far. This date was absolutely in the spontaneous spirit of My Groupon Adventure. I was still doing something adventurous and weird. But this time I was sharing it with someone and consequently enjoying it so much more. When Alex returned, conversation turned to my project and the gamut of deals. I told her about the alligators, about my bolthole on Mars, and everything else too. Yet she seemed to have done more Groupon deals than me. This date was just the tip of the iceberg. It seemed I had finally met my match.

Alex was puckish and boisterous, which I liked. She said, 'I had a wax on Groupon. Never again: it was agony. They actually took some skin off. I said *"I want you to get rid of my pubes, not my clitoris!"'* This was my sort of girl. We talked for hours and hours. Comfortably outlasting Simon, who headed home. Probably to regale his wife with the walrus impression that he'd doubtless stolen from my cache of fail-proof seduction techniques. Conversation gushed unbidden. At one point Alex told me she thought I was, quote, *'so interesting'*. She was very pissed, admittedly. And she had just ripped eyeholes in a napkin and then worn it like a burka. But she still said it. And that innocuous sounding sentence felt like a significant moment for me. Because I realised that I'd thought I was boring because Jen *made me feel boring*. Alex is into astronomy. She told me that there are a hundred million stars in our galaxy, but only 5,000 are visible to the naked eye. For the rest we need a telescope. In the same way, as individuals we only have access to a fraction of ourselves. And so, no wonder we think we're boring: there's a galaxy of memories, opinions and thoughts we can't see with our own eyes. We can only access them through other people. And that's what I think love is. Love is like a telescope.

We were the last people left in the restaurant. And we had been for the best part of an hour. The staff had stacked the chairs on the tables, taken off their uniforms, and were now turning off the lights. It was time to go. 'Do you fancy having one more drink?' I said. 'Yeah. That would be great,' she said, stumbling out of the door. We walked down through Leicester Square to a small bar I knew stayed open till late. We strode past a huge queue snaking out of Tiger Tiger. Doe-eyed drunk singletons teetered, all waiting to pawn their dignity to pay the debt of their own loneliness. Tiger Tiger: a Narnia of orifices all waiting for tenants. I was so glad not to be in there. Selling myself on Groupon was a contrived and convoluted way to find love, but it was easier than a nightclub. The sun had begun to rise by the time we called it a night. 'So … would you like to do this again?' I asked tentatively. I'd never repeated a Groupon before. But I knew that this adventure was only just beginning. 'I'd love to,' she said. Then – in the interests of full disclosure, dear reader – there was heavy petting. Which is kissing, but a level of kissing that would be inappropriate in a swimming pool. And it was bloody excellent.

Chapter Eighteen

It seemed an entirely appropriate activity for our second date. She loved Groupon, I loved Groupon. It was irreverent and silly. We'd get to visit parts of London we'd never normally get to see. It was the perfect choice. So I was feeling rather smug as I walked through London Waterloo station. We'd arranged to meet under the clock. I'd been looking forward to our reunion ever since I kissed her goodnight in Leicester Square. And I was even more nervous the second time round, which was a sure sign that I was into her. But she was going to absolutely love this date. I was sure of it. We spotted one another and embraced. Then I broke the good news. 'Is this some sort of joke?' she said. This wasn't the reaction I'd been expecting. 'Tell me this is a wind-up? How is this a suitable thing to do on a date?' 'I wanted to do something a bit different,' I explained. 'And so you chose a guided tour of London's best toilets?' 'Exactly,' I said. 'Now follow me. We're meeting the rest of the tour party outside Costa.'

There were 15 other people in our group. Although notably no other couples on a date. Which meant that I was obviously the only man creative enough to think of it. What can I say? I'm a hopeless romantic. We set off for our first toilet. Sulking at the back of our posse, Alex had an inexorable frown stuck to her face. 'At least it's not raining!' I japed. It immediately started to rain. 'Oh well,' I said, 'the tour only takes three hours.' 'Three fucking hours!' Alex could be quite scary when she was angry. Our first destination was the jewel in London's lavatory crown, the Diamond Jubiloo. Stationed on the South Bank, it costs 50p to use, but my God it's worth it. It was built in homage to Her Majesty to mark her Diamond Jubilee. Why anyone thought this was appropriate we'll never know. The Queen probably had to open it too. But I suppose nothing could be as bad at the Keswick pencil museum. The Jubiloo is regally decked out. Inside it's positively plush: the toilet seats are designed to look like Union Jacks; the cleaners are dressed as Beefeaters; it's even got its own special royal toilet paper. Accept no imitations. If in doubt, hold a sheet up to the light: you should be able to see the Queen's face. 'Why don't you give it a test drive?' I said to Alex, trying to inject some fun into proceedings. I presented her with a fifty pence piece. 'My treat.' 'I don't need the toilet,' she said. 'You can't even squeeze out a little wee?' I said. 'No,' she said sharply.

Our group was led all over town by Sophie, an American drama student and part-time morris dancer. Sophie held a toilet plunger proudly above her head throughout. A sort of lavatorial North Star, which we followed obediently. It was like we were part of some bizarre toilet cult. At one point we passed the London Scientology headquarters, and even they rolled their eyes. 'Weirdos,' heckled one of them, taking a moment's rest from handing out leaflets claiming that humans had evolved from clams. Sophie told us that an average person spends a year and half on the toilet in their life. That's a very long time. Which is why I always take care to multitask on the loo by either reading, replying to e-mails, or crying. I once had a poo whilst eating a bag of pretzels. I just thought, this is the circle of life. The year and a half on the toilet figure seems very long in hindsight. I imagine that if you take dads out of the figures, then the average probably comes down to about three months. Alex had stopped listening by this point though. And was now talking to her mother on the phone. No doubt giving me rave reviews.

Fifteen epic bogs later, we ended the tour at an underground cocktail bar on The Strand. Essentially the pre-internet Grindr – in a previous life this was the infamous public toilet where Oscar Wilde and chums would assemble to joust quills. By now we were all totally drenched. But as Alex vacuumed a mojito, her wet hair glued to her cheeks, the misery finally evaporated from her face. 'That was a really crap choice for a date,' she said. 'I'm sorry,' I said, 'I thought you'd be into it.' 'You thought I'd be into toilets?' 'Something like that.' 'I'm not.' 'Well, it's the thought that counts.' 'Yes. You're right. What a sweet thought. But I think I'll arrange the next one.' At this stage, I was delighted that there was even going to be a next one. I was beginning to have my doubts. 'Fair enough!' I said. 'When are you next free?' 'Well, what are you doing tomorrow afternoon?' she said. 'There's a cat cafe that's opened in East London that I really want to try.'

And so that's where we went. Lady Dinah's Cat Cafe in Shoreditch. Essentially this is a normal cafe, but with lots of cats mincing about like aloof French jazz musicians. There are about 12 cats in total. To be honest, I was disappointed by that. I thought there'd be a lot more. I basically thought I'd be walking around the cafe wearing a suit of cats. But no, there were only a dozen felines, and most of them were asleep. Which I thought was poor form. These cats are basically sort of cat prostitutes. And so I expected them to paint on a smile, slip on their slinkiest bikini, and sell their wares a little bit. But most of them just lay there, supine in their bed. It was like having coffee on a coma ward. (*Now, that really would be a bad date choice.*) But finally one of the cats woke up and wandered over. It then winked at me, as if to say 'Shhhh! I'm actually a dog', and from that point on I fell in love with the place.

Alex was in her element. She was having a smashing time. But to be fair anything was an improvement on toilets. We could have gone rambling in Chernobyl and it still would have represented a better day out. We sat down at a table and immediately fell deep into conversation. Spending time with Alex felt as natural as breathing. Everything was so easy. The waitress delivered a cream tea to our table. I began to smother a scone in strawberry jam. 'So what made you start this whole Groupon thing?' she said, 'I've been meaning to ask.' 'Faith,' I said. 'I was inspired by faith.' 'As in, what? Religious faith? I didn't put you down as the sort.' 'No. Not at all. I am definitely not religious in the slightest. Very much cool with sex before marriage, for example.' 'Well, that's a huge weight off my mind,' she said with heavy sarcasm. 'I suppose what I mean by "faith" is that at some point I realised that what I'd done previously in my life didn't have to equal what I could do in the future.' 'OK …' she said. 'Basically, I think too often we let the evidence thrown up by our lives decide our next move. And that evidence makes that choice feel logical and correct but it's so limiting. The truth is that we really can do anything we want.' 'Wow. Deep' she said, only slightly less sarcastically.

'My point is that we think of the choices available to us in our life as a tree diagram narrowly branching off from our current situation. But that's a dangerous illusion. In reality our choices are infinite. A kaleidoscope of possibility waiting for us to take a chance. And all we need is imagination.' 'I didn't realise I was going out with the fifteen-year-old Alain de Botton,' she said. 'It takes a lifetime to peel this onion,' I said, before biting into a scone. 'But what does all that have to do with faith?' she said. 'Well, what is imagination? It's an act of faith, surely? Faith that's there's an abundance of potential in the world waiting for us to dare to look for it.' I was in a quixotic mood. But it's hard to look serious and philosophical when there's a kitten climbing all over your face.

On the train back from Shoreditch it dawned on me that love is about faith too. Well, perhaps not love, but falling in love at least. Love reproduces asexually. It replenishes and expands all by itself. But getting there, actually falling in love, requires time and energy. And you don't invest that time in someone if you don't believe you could love them. So I wasn't in love with Alex. Not yet. It was still very early days. But somehow I knew it was a matter of time. She was someone I could imagine being in love with. So I felt in the process of falling in love, which was an odd state to be in. It was strange to be so self-aware. Stuck in the whirlpool but dissociated from it too. Drowning in it but also looking down upon it from a great height. I wasn't in love, and I wasn't out of love, I was in limbo. I felt like a diver, who having been trapped inside a deep-sea wreckage, had now finally fought free and was rocketing towards the surface. Seeking out the oxygen and the light.

Alex and I saw each other five nights out of seven. Philippa and Hope had advised me to take things slow, but I didn't see the point. If something works, why hesitate? We went for dinner. We went to the theatre. We went to the London Aquarium. We had a picnic under the setting sun in Greenwich Park. And then I took her to bingo. This was the last Groupon voucher I had left. And I was sure we'd be swept up in the nostalgic charm of the kitsch entertainment. This time I made sure I'd done my research. I didn't want a repeat of the toilet tour fiasco. I texted Alex with my plan and she said she actually *loved* bingo. It was hard to know if she was telling the truth. I'd told her on our first date that I loved opera, and I was definitely lying. But on a sticky Friday evening we headed off to Tooting and bingo is exactly what we did. And I had a great time. So good, in fact, that I actually popped the question.

When Alex told me she had both a Gala Bingo and a Mecca Bingo membership card I'd assumed it was a joke. She's an advertising creative and it's the sort of thing a hipster like her might have. I thought it was probably just another bit of ironic plumage in her increasingly meta-life. Along with the vintage bike, passion for craft stout, and nerdy T-shirt with the slogan 'Science gives me a Hadron'. Some people are so cool they're no longer sure where the joke ends and their personality begins. They exist as a post-modern melange, not remembering what parts of their self are authentic and what bits are just taking the piss. I'd personally never been to bingo. I had heard of it. But in the same way that I'd heard of unicorns or Penge. Always assuming it to be a myth. Or at least something from another time that had slowly become extinct. Like Syphilis, or *Grandstand*, or Craig David.

The queue at reception was massive: I'd clearly underestimated bingo's popularity. We eventually made it into the hall, which was unnecessarily ornate: a baroque theatre over two levels. Suggesting that bingo used to be a big deal in the distant past but was now in decline. It was like going to your nan's house and seeing a photo of her from the 1950s, dressed in a ballgown, looking really hot. The circle wasn't open tonight, so we were sat on the huge bottom floor, a sea of tables spread symmetrically across a blue carpet that smelt of stale lager. The patrons sat bent over their fat books, marker pens poised. All of them old and withered, sheaved in mackintoshes, downing cheap rosé. It was like a zombie apocalypse episode of *Last of the Summer Wine*.

On a stage at the front of the room stood the caller, sounding jaded as he pursed the numbers from his orange face. 'All the threes, 33.' He said. But in a tone of voice that suggested he was actually saying, 'All the threes, 33. I went to RADA, you know? And now I'm doing this shit.' 'Full house!' screamed an old woman – inducing waves of tortured, angry groans from the thwarted throngs. With loud tutting and whispered conspiracy theories. '*She always wins that woman. I heard she had it off with the caller.*' '*Yeah. She's in that wheelchair, but my friend Sonia said she saw her doing a handstand in Greggs.*' After seven rounds I hadn't won a thing. Not a penny. Alex, however, was rolling in it. She flicked a twenty at me from across the table and told me to get a round of drinks. 'Thanks Mum,' I said. I didn't mind though. I would need some Dutch courage for what I was about to do. I ordered a pint of lager, rum and coke, and a packet of crisps. 'That will be £4.80, please,' he said. It was like I'd quantum-leaped back to the eighties.

I put the drinks down on the table where Alex was working her way through a thick wad of scratch cards. I swiftly downed half my pint. 'Alex?' I said. 'Mmmmm?' Alex didn't look up. 'I've got something I want to ask you.' 'Mmmmm. Great. OH FUCK!' 'What's the matter?' I said. 'I almost won a car.' 'Oh. Right. Cool. I almost won a cat once.' 'What do you mean?' 'Nothing. Now, you can say "no" if you want. Obviously. I know it's early days for me to ask you this, but ...' 'Spit it out. The bingo is re-starting in a minute,' 'Well, I just wondered, basically, if ...ummm ... you might like to be my "plus one" for my cousin's wedding?' 'Yeah sure. Fine. Whatever. I'm going for a wee,' she said, standing up.

'Sorry?' 'I said I'm going for a wee'. 'You don't think it's weird?' 'No? I've been for a wee pretty much every day of my life?' 'No. I mean the wedding thing. You don't think it's too much too soon?' 'No. It's fine. I love weddings. It's not a big deal. Look, I'm bursting. If the bloke comes around again can you get me some more scratch cards?'

I was delighted. Alex had saved me from humiliation: I could now fulfil my promise of having a date for the wedding. But her nonchalant acceptance was also a sure sign she liked me as much as I liked her. The pressure was off. I felt exquisitely relaxed. I picked up my phone to text Mum the good news. I knew she'd be as excited as me about my blossoming romance. I took a sip of my beer and thought about the ridiculous snake of dominos that had fallen for me to reach this point. Mum texted back straight away. 'It better not be a hooker.' I laughed out loud. My mum has such a good sense of humour! My phone buzzed again. 'I'm not even joking.' Charming. As if I'd bring a prostitute to my cousin's wedding ... there was no way I could afford an escort on my salary! Alex sat back down and the bitter caller returned to his microphone. I was as unsuccessful in the second half as I had been in the first. But I didn't care. Life had never been better.

Chapter Nineteen

The big day had arrived. This afternoon I would finally head to my cousin's wedding with Alex on my arm. I was actually looking forward to it now. Describing the beautiful terror of falling in love is like trying to catch a tornado in a plastic bag. But it felt like I'd had a blood transfusion and been given the blood of a man three times my size. My body pulsed with oxygen. They say that in love you seek your other half. You seek your shadow: those qualities that you lack in yourself. And in her cheerfulness, self-confidence and impish energy I saw a better version of me. And those were the winds that I longed to sail forwards on, into our imagined future. I could physically feel myself being enlarged; inflated like a balloon by her ideas. In life we are faced with an enormous wall of doors. Like an advent calendar. Little hatches to different worlds. Different paths. Different answers. Experience flings opens some of these gates. But vast swathes remain locked. Yet love is both a key and a torchlight. And through the new people with whom we become hopelessly entangled, new possibilities are lit up. And that felt wonderful.

There was a chance that I was being totally deluded, of course. But I didn't mind. Mendacity can be useful sometimes. I love those 'Missed Connections' features you see in newspapers. Where people plead for strangers they have seen on the tube to come forward and be reunited with them. '*You got on at Waterloo. I had Nutella on my face. Your dog bit a child. You could be the one*.' Or '*It was the District Line. I was eating cottage cheese with my hands. You were on fire. We shared a moment.*' Or '*It was on the platform at Leicester Square. You had a flag. I was blacked-up. Is it too good to be true?*' There's an inspiring naivety to these people. A heroic delusion. If I truly was being deluded, then I was glad. All greatness is a story of delusion because greatness looks like futility until it happens.

'How do I look?' I said, stood in the hallway at the flat. 'Quite handsome actually,' said Phil. 'Well, there's a first time for everything,' smiled Hope. 'Do Groupon sell plastic surgery now or something?' I adjusted the waistcoat on my morning suit. The sound of a car horn announced that the cab was outside. I met Alex on the platform at Clapham Junction train station. She looked perfectly elegant in her blue dress. We had agreed to have a drink with my parents in a pub opposite Dorking station. As we walked in, my father ostentatiously rubbed his eyes as if he couldn't believe what he was seeing. Alex laughed politely. That's the thing with going out with me, you will become very good at feigning mirth. Dad then began to pinch his face. 'Just want to check I'm not dreaming!' he said. This was classic Dad. He always flirts with my girlfriends. 'So, you must be Alex!' He said, holding out his hand. 'Much better looking than the last one!' My dad ran over to the window. 'Jonathan, what on earth are you doing?' said my mother, seriously embarrassed. 'Just checking the sky for flying pigs!' he said. I rolled my eyes. I was in for a whole day of this.

Meanwhile, Dave was sound checking at the reception venue. My phone buzzed with a text message. 'Venue won't let us use the laser show or smoke machine. Some bullshit about epileptics. I'm absolutely furious.' After a sharpener in the pub, we got a cab to the church. Mum and Dad went inside to find a seat. But we were 20 minutes early, so Alex and I had a stroll around the grounds. We found an old bench looking over the pretty cemetery. It was a fine summer's day filled with the most intense light. The air looked more transparent than I'd ever seen. 'I've got something to give you,' she said, reaching into her handbag. 'I've got us two tickets for the opera next month.' 'Oh brilliant!' I said. 'You know me! I *love* the opera.' 'I've got something for you too actually,' I said. I retrieved an A4 certificate that I'd folded in half and kept in my jacket pocket. 'What is it?' she said, studying it in her hands. 'I've bought you a star,' I said. And I genuinely had. I was loath to line the pockets of Dennis Hope with any more of my precious cash, but he had a total monopoly of space, and it's not like I could switch to a fair trade supplier. So for what I promise was my last ever Groupon deal I'd bought Alex an actual, real star. 'It's named after you,' I said, 'I thought you might be able to look for it with your telescope.' 'That's the cheesiest thing anyone has ever done,' she said. 'But I love it. Thank you.'

We took our position in the church and saw my cousin tie the knot. The reception was at a golf club down the road. I was deliberately seated next to Dave's father, Dennis, at dinner, because he didn't know anyone else. He was an old family friend, by which I mean he was a drunken liability who'd only been invited out of politeness. I'd been ordered to keep my eye on him throughout the evening. I don't think I'd seen him smile since his divorce from Dave's mother a decade previously. 'What you up to these days, Dennis?' I asked, as we both tentatively poked at a goat's cheese tart. 'You enjoying your retirement?' 'I've taken up metal-detecting,' he said. 'Oh great! That sounds like fun!' I said. 'Not really. It's just a relentless trawling through nothingness,' he said. I downed my entire glass of wine and immediately topped myself up again. This was going to be a long evening.

Dennis is a conversation sponge. One of these people with an amazing capacity to absorb all the questions you ask them without giving you anything back whatsoever. 'So are you courting at the moment, Dennis?' I asked, with bated breath. 'I am as it goes,' he said. 'I've gone on a couple of dates with this widow I met on Guardian Soulmates. You know that dating site which the Ipswich strangler was on? 'That's great news,' I said. 'Yes, it's gone quite well,' he continued. 'On the first date she said I was a brilliant listener, or something. And then she had me round for dinner last night. Lovely place she's got. I had a bit of a nose about. Lots of photos of her late husband. He's no great shakes in the looks department, and I'm definitely taller. Also, he's dead, so I've got an edge there.' I nodded along warmly. 'Well I hope it all works out,' I said. 'Let me tell you about hope,' he said. 'Hope is like having great foreplay with an impotent man.' I was so glad that Dennis wasn't making a speech.

It was time to cut the wedding cake. The faces of the bride and groom were nowhere to be seen on it, which I thought was a wasted opportunity. The first dance was meant to be 'Think About Me' by Fleetwood Mac. But nobody had told Fleetwood Snack this crucial information, because they played 'Go Your Own Way' instead. The first line of which is, 'Loving you isn't the right thing to do'. Not exactly the perfect message for newly-weds. Anyway, Dave and his friends played it brilliantly. In fact, the whole set was a huge success. I'd never seen him happier, and I was so glad. Because without Dave I would not have been dancing here with Alex. He lit the fuse. Moments have doors we need to walk though. And sometimes we need help to make that decision. Someone to shove us off the cliff, so we might dive into the possibility. Dave had been that person for me. I knew My Groupon Adventure was down to him.

When Fleetwood Snack had finished their triumphant set, I found Dennis at the bar. As expected, he was absolutely hammered. 'Did you get them a wedding present then?' he slurred. 'Yes,' I said, 'I got them a fondue set.' 'Groupon?' he said. 'Obviously. Did you get them something?' 'I gave them a vintage gold locket,' he said. 'Wow. Dennis. That's very generous,' I said, taken aback. 'I found it on the beach,' he said. 'Right,' I said. That made much more sense. 'It's a funny thing metal-detecting,' said Dennis. 'You can spend year after year, going out day after day, for hours on end and find absolutely nothing. And then one day, out of the blue you din the most beautiful thing you've ever seen.' Alex had joined me now, clutching two more glasses of white wine. 'Dennis, I know exactly what you mean.'

Epilogue

And so that was the story of how Groupon changed my life. You might be wondering what happened next? Well, firstly, after the wedding, I decided to leave the world of Groupon behind once and for all. I hope you don't feel let down. I did it for Alex's sake mainly. I'd had my fun. I'd transformed myself as I'd desperately needed to. Now it was time to put my Groupon toy back in the box and move on. However, let's not beat around the bush: I failed. I can't deny that. I had lost my bet with Dave. I promised to do 52 weeks of Groupons and I packed it all in at week 40. Admittedly I had done over 100 Groupons by this stage when you agglomerate all those bought for me and the mindless splurge during my addiction phase. But I hadn't abided by the rules and therefore I'd invoked the Groupon from Hell punishment. I nervously anticipated my penance.

Dave made me wait a long time for it. Until the evening of my twenty-seventh birthday to be exact. It was a symbolic choice: the day that could have been my coronation as King of the Spontaneous, had I not thrown in the towel. We met outside Bethnal Green tube station. I heard Dave before I saw him. Nobody else would have been whistling the *Baywatch* theme tune. He had a rapturous smile bursting out of his face. 'You're going to really hate this!' he said, gleefully. 'Follow me'. For the next 20 minutes we mooned around the benighted backstreets of Bethnal Green. I definitely recognised this place – but from where? Eventually we came to a small church hall.

'This is it', said Dave. 'I've been here before, haven't I?' I said. Dave nodded. 'We both have.' 'But when?' I asked. 'Life drawing class. Remember?' 'Oh yes!' I said, 'With that bonkers guy! The model. What was his name … ?' 'Paul.' 'Yes! Paul!' I said. We walked up the concrete steps. I was amazed that this was the punishment he'd chosen. I thought Dave was a lot crueller than that. Remember this was the same guy that tried to get me circumcised on our trip to America. But it was my birthday. And so maybe he'd decided to water his retribution down and just be nice? We went inside.

'Great to see you again!' said Keith, the head honcho, welcoming us warmly. 'Yes, it's good to be back', I said. 'I'm looking forward to catching up with Paul.' 'Unfortunately Paul can't make it tonight', said Keith. 'Oh that's a shame!' I said. 'Thanks so much for stepping into the breach though, Max', said Keith. 'I really appreciate it.' I laughed but Keith stared back at me blankly. 'You can get changed in the kitchen if you like?' he said. 'Yes, chop, chop', said Dave. 'Sorry. What do you mean?' I asked. 'We start in 10 minutes', said Keith, quickly walking off to tend to another customer. 'Dave', I said. 'You absolute bastard!' Dave hadn't diluted his revenge at all! He'd concentrated it into one last almighty humiliation. I thought about doing a runner. But rules is rules. Dave wouldn't let this lie. If I refused this punishment he'd only come up with something even worse. And so I did as I was told, getting changed next to the fridge before shuffling out in just my boxers.

'Ladies and gentleman, this is Max', said Keith. The audience applauded thinly. They were arranged in a wide circle all around me. So every inch of my blemished body was up for scrutiny. I awkwardly peeled off my pants. This was the most excruciating part. When the mendacious fantasy of what my body looks like collided with the cold hard facts. I'm not grotesque by any means. It would be disingenuous for me to say that I am. But I certainly looked lived-in, put it that way. By which I mean dilapidated, not pregnant.

'Perhaps you'd like to take your first pose?' suggested Keith, politely. 'If I'd known I was going to get lucky tonight I would have tidied myself up!' I quipped into the abyss. No one laughed. No one was even listening. They were just staring intently. Many holding their thumb up for perspective. I put my hands on my waist like Superman, and stared out of the window eager to avoid all eye contact. But then I came to a comforting realisation: these artists were here to draw, not to degrade. I was simply an object to be contemplated and then translated onto paper. And at least my indignity was contained. My humiliation was isolated to this room and this moment. Two hours later I'd be back in the anonymity of the night and all would be forgotten. I allowed myself to smile.

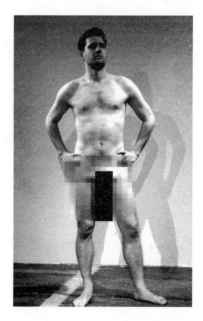

As soon as I'd finished this soothing thought a gang of teenagers appeared at a window at the back of the hall. They hollered and pointed. '*Oh my daaaayyssss! Wat a waste-man!*' said one, in absolute hysterics. '*Oi fam! Look at dis paedo!*' shouted another. Their laughter was riotous. A black wall of camera phones were suddenly and simultaneously raised to the glass. Flash. And with that my shame was saved for posterity.

Dave had got me pretty good. But I deserved that, I suppose. He was just imposing the rules that I myself had agreed to. When class had finished and I'd got dressed once more, we shook hands outside the hall. We were fair and square. My dignity may have taken a dive but my integrity was still intact and that was the important thing. I actually didn't mind this final embarrassment. On balance My Groupon Adventure had been a huge success. I was a better man and I'd met a girl I loved. Which brings me to the final question: what of my blossoming relationship with Alex? I'll leave that up to your imagination. But what I will say is that I did buy this:

Acknowledgements

This book could not have happened without the help and collaboration of a lot of people. First and foremost, I am hugely grateful to everyone who pledged on Unbound. Feel free to come up to me in the pub and badger me for a free drink at some point. Or ask me to sponsor you to run the bloody marathon. At Unbound I've received great support from Mathew Clayton, Caitlin Harvey, Georgia Odd, Emily Shipp and many more. But I'd particularly like to thank my editor, Phil Connor, who has tirelessly responded to my tsunami of ridiculous e-mails, which often had subject headings like: "Is the phrase 'Guess the weight of the asylum seeker' racist?"

Outside of Unbound, I'd like to thank Dave (obviously), Alex (ditto), Karen Reed (you don't know how important you were), and Simon Woodsford. Ben Wilson directed my Edinburgh show, but his advice on structure transferred to the book too. I owe a debt to friends who have read and given notes on various drafts including Philippa Berry, Max Whitehead, and Timon Woodward. Finally, I'd like to thank Becky Williams at DAA Management (she's the one to contact in the inevitable event that you'd like to buy the film rights); my parents, Jonathan and Belinda Dickins, who were relentlessly supportive; and anyone who has posted an inspirational quote on Facebook at any stage in the process.

Subscribers

Unbound is a new kind of publishing house. Our books are funded directly by readers. This was a very popular idea during the late eighteenth and early nineteenth centuries. Now we have revived it for the internet age. It allows authors to write the books they really want to write and readers to support the writing they would most like to see published.

The names listed below are of readers who have pledged their support and made this book happen. If you'd like to join them, visit: www.unbound.co.uk.

Ronni Adams
Malek Adjerad
António Albuquerque
Henry Algeo
Paul Andreas
Igor Andronov
Sara Attwood
Oliver Barnes
Nick Baucher
James bavister
Marisa Bavister
Ed Ben
Nicholas Berman
Philippa Berry
Helen Birchenough
Jonathan Bloom
Nathan Bloomfield

Faye Boakes
Andy Bracken
Stephen Bradley
Andy Bradnam
Jeremy Brecknock
Sonia Brecknock
Paul Bruce
Daniel Burgess
Gordon Butler
Andy & Joy Candler
Maria Carvalho
Rick Challener
Yosi Chandler
Penny Charnaud
Andrew Checker
Angie Chiswell
Em Clark

Matthew Clark
Louisa Codd
Michele Cohen
Olivia Cole
Gemma Coles
Philip Connor
Rachel Cooper
Jennifer Crompton
Nick Crompton
John Cunningham
Rebecca Darmody
Luca de Bants
Hardeep Deol
Ben Dickins
Jonathan Dickins
Lulu Dickins
Iain Dockery

Sarah Dorin
Jenny Doughty
Hilary Dowling
Justine Ducros
Kelly Dudley
Vivienne Dunstan
Matthew Eastaugh
Rob Edmunds
Christophe Elisha
Charlotte Endersby
Lilach Epstein
Anne Evans
Nicky Evelegh
Colin Failes
Paul Flower
Sam Floy
Jane Forbes
Colin Forrest-Charde
Paul Fox
Isobel Frankish
Jez Franks
Alice Gamm
Louise Garnham
Jonathan Gershfield
Nigel Gilbert-Harris
James Gill
Kate Girardot
Bryan Goldsmith
Roberta Goodhead
David Goodier
Edward Gotham
Keith Grady
David Gunner
Samantha Hall
Fairlie Hamilton
Sally Hardie
Jane Hardisty
Marc Hardman
Paul Harris
Caitlin Harvey
Chris Hassan
Paul Hawkins
Andrew Hearse
Colin Hill

Yannick Hill
Anton Hong
Liz Howe
Luci Humphreys
Meredith Hurst
Sarah Hymans
Deb Ikin
Tim Iles
Johari Ismail
Chantel James
Laura Jellicoe
Frances Jeune
Caz Johnson
Louise Jones
Oliver Judge
Mary Kauffman
Charlotte Kaye
Andy Keelaghan
Karen Keppler
Sajeela Kershi
Dan Kieran
Alex Kirk
Ryan Kirkhoff
Penny Lakin
Thomas Lancaster
Stephen Leach
Darren Lean
Gareth Lean
Rich Legate
Kevin Little
Kimberley Lucas
Eleonore Lurie
Seonaid Mackenzie-
    Murray
Karen Macleod
Heather Marchant
Jill Marshall
Shaun McAlister
Lauren McKeown
Steven McKinnon
Leslie Merritt
Peter Milburn
Vicky Mills
John Mitchinson

Jaydip D Modhwadia - The
    Almighty Kid!
Zsa Moncreiffe
Karen Morden
Victoria Mossop
Liane Mount
Sarah Mumby
Alanah Murphy
Emma Murphy
Carlo Navato
Wilfred Ng
Jennifer Nicholas
Andrew Nowson
Finn Nuallain
Rob O'Donovan
Georgia Odd
Sue Parker
Sarah Patmore
Sally Peck
Nigel Pennington
Eve Perry
Seva Phillips
André Pinto
Gabriel Pollard
Justin Pollard
Daniel Potter
Donna Potter
Jean Power
Janet Pretty
Lawrence Pretty
Rhian Heulwen Price
Kitt Proudfoot
Nigel Quinnen
Ramsay Family
Mala Rastogi
Nicola Reid
Craig Reilly
Ben Rogers
Mark Rosser
Alex Royston
Zhenya Rozidor
Sally Russell
Debra Ryland
Satwant S.K.

Neil A Scales
Peter Schooling
John Sheehan
Sukie Shinn
David Simpson
Alice Smith
Eggzy Smith
Mark Smith
Nic Smith
The Smixons
Jonny Snelling
Mary Anne St Clair-Ford
Katie Steingold
Jason Stevens
Kelly Stevens
Martin Stewart
Felix Taylor
Jayne Thomas
Jenna Thomas
Katherine-Louvain
  Thompson
Amanda Thurman
Sarah Tilley
Julia Tratt
Niall Urquhart
Kati Vallius
David Van De Wiel
Elizabeth Van Pelt
Nicholas Vandy
Mark Vent
Rob Waite
Claire Walker
Berent Wallendahl
Caroline Walsh
Ruihua Wang
Kirsty Warriss
Holly Watson
Lou Watson
James Watts
Runa Way
Max Wegner
Louise Welch
David Westendorp
Helen Wharton

Bettie White
Max Whitehead
Ben Whitehouse
Angela Wiggan
Patrick Wilcox
Dave Williams
Ben Wilson
Derek Wilson
Mark Wilson
Adrian Windsor
Andy Winter
Damian Woolfe
Dan Wright
Fabiana Xavier
David Yarnold
Ian Young
Peter Young
Tom Ziessen

R